The Compact Book of
FRESH WATER
FISHING

Edited by Bob Zwirz

Contributors

Bob Zwirz   Grits Gresham

Ray Ovington   Milt Tosko

Jack Seville   Tom McNally

J. LOWELL PRATT & COMPANY
Publishers   New York

Grateful acknowledgement is made to the various boat and tackle
manufacturers whose products are pictured in this book. Many
thanks go to the authors who have supplied their own photographs
and those photographs from their files.

Published by J. Lowell Pratt & Company, New York and on the
same day by The Clark Company, Toronto, Canada.

The volumes in The American Sports Library are nationally distributed by The Kable News Company, New York.

PREFACE

This book, together with the other volumes in THE COMPACT OUTDOORSMAN'S LIBRARY, was created to fill a large gap in the literature of outdoor recreational sports and hobbies.

Americans are more outdoor conscious than ever before but many are woefully unprepared when they take to the open. Through their lack of knowledge of proper equipment and basic information they may miss the pleasures to which they are entitled, encounter dissappointment, trouble and even danger.

These books, written and edited by a board of highly respected experts in their favorite fields of interest, mark a new high in editorial concept that is not content with just one man's opinion. Thus the reader receives concise and accurate advice from many sources. The seasoned sportsman can secure new information and the beginner will experience the excitement of a new sport and learn its basic fundamentals.

Although no book can present any subject complete in all its varied aspects, THE COMPACT OUTDOORSMAN'S LIBRARY provides an authoritative starting point. The bibliography at the end of the books lists sources of more specialized information.

The publishers hope that you will keep this book for ready reference. Carry it in the glove compartment, the tackle box or in your sporting jacket.

Ray Ovington

INTRODUCTION

By Bob Zwirz

It's near inconceivable to many foreigners that we in the United States have such an interesting variety of fishing—mostly all of it, free!

One of the greatest assets of our democratic ideology lies in the fact that thousands of miles of rivers and streams are kept open to public angling. The same is true of the majority of our lakes and impoundments. In a nation where recreation claims such a large segment of each family's free time, it is not surprising that fishing has become the number one participation sport.

According to a recent national survey made by the United States Fish and Wildlife Service, some 30,000,000 Americans are interested in this great outdoor pastime.

The "Compact Book of Fresh Water Fishing" has been written to give this vast audience an overall view of the opportunities that await the more informed and versatile outdoorsman and his family. As in any sport, it will be the skilled performer that will reap the greatest rewards, and in so doing have the most fun.

Each chapter of this book deals with a segment of fishing, from its history in America to the more complex subject of tackle and its usage. Most important, we discuss the more sought after species of fish and the most productive methods for catching them. And, these widely-read writers will reveal some of their favorite fishing grounds so that you too may share in the enjoyment of America's top spots.

These authors, chosen for their expert knowledge and deep love of the sport, represent the best in their field. Each man has spent a lifetime learning to understand the rivers and lakes of his part of the country and the ways of the fish that inhabit them. Most have fished this entire country at one time or another and some go as far afield as Africa, South America and the limestone streams of the England of Marryatt and Halford.

It is our profound hope that when you have finished reading this book you will have gained some knowledge, and the desire to experience it all, yourself. For it is in the doing that we are able to build experience, and experience, you will find, is the all-important key to skill.

THE CONTENTS

Page

Preface, by Ray Ovington   5

Introduction, by Bob Zwirz   6

CHAPTER I
ANGLING IN AMERICA, by Bob Zwirz   11

CHAPTER II
TROUT AND THE ATLANTIC SALMON,
by Bob Zwirz   19

CHAPTER III
STEELHEAD AND PACIFIC SALMON ANGLING,
by Ray Ovington   35

CHAPTER IV
BASS, PIKE, AND MUSKELLUNGE FISHING,
by Tom McNally   43

CHAPTER V
HOW TO USE YOUR TACKLE,
by Grits Gresham   53

CHAPTER VI
TACKLE TALK, by Milt Rosko   60

CHAPTER VII
FRESH-WATER FISHING—WHEN AND WHERE,
by Jack Seville   74

GLOSSARY   94

BIBLIOGRAPHY   95

INDEX   96

The Compact Book
of Fresh Water Fishing

CHAPTER I

ANGLING IN AMERICA

By Bob Zwirz

We've come to think of fishing as a sport and that is as it should be! But it wasn't considered a sport, in America, back in the days of our first settlers. Fish were considered a survival item and as an aid to soil fertilization.

There are records showing that as far back as the Third Century A.D. someone had the ingenuity to fashion an artificial fly made of feathers and hook that produced the desired result. It caught fish! And, methods of casting a line, by hand, were far from unknown in the days of the Pharaohs of Egypt. So too was the art of the circular casting net.

Books have been passed down to us from the England of the 1600's that have made it quite clear angling in the British Isles reached a stage of development far more advanced than most of us might imagine.

But it was not until the mid-1800's that angling became anything near the sport as we think of it these days. Credit goes to a small group of dedicated individuals of that era, rather than to an industry or to any co-ordinated mass thinking on the subject. It is interesting to examine documents of that period and to be able to trace the evolution of fishing, especially in America, first as a means toward an end and then, slowly but surely, as a sport to look forward to in our leisure moments.

The first strides in the field of American sport fishing took place in the field of "bait-casting" and it took place, for the most part, down South. Back around 1809, in the state of Kentucky, there lived a clever, dedicated bass angler by the name of George Snyder. Ofttimes, while fishing with other members of the famous old "Bourbon Angling Club," of which he was president, he wished to have a more practical way of working the line—both when casting the bait and while playing the fish. Being a watchmaker by trade, he was just the man to devise the first workable multiplying reel.

By 1840 others had seen the new invention, perfected it and started the first manufacturing of fishing reels in America. The factory was operated by two brothers, B. F. and J. F. Meek of Frankfort, Ky.

Through the years, changes have occurred that have made the bait-casting reel a joy to use and practically free of the old problem of back-lash, at least while in reasonably skilled hands. The design is still basically the same.

While America was becoming aware of fishing as relaxation and as a sport, there were great strides being made in England by the advocates of the fly rod. More has been learned and recorded by the fly-fishing fraternity than some are willing to admit. In many ways, the dyed-in-the-wool fly-fisherman is the statistician of fresh water angling! Part entomologist, part ichthyologist and most assuredly equal parts of wisdom, curiosity and patience go into the general make-up of the skilled angler who fishes with the fly and the fly alone.

Probably the greatest arguments concerning tackle of the mid-1800's took place over the merits of various woods to be used in the making of fly rods. For years there were preferences for greenheart wood, or sometimes lancewood or Bethabora as a substance for making up the long, parabolic sticks of that day. However, William Mitchell, a tackle pioneer of that era reported in "The American Angler" that a man by the name of William Blacker of Soho, London, England, made up a split bamboo fly rod for an American, James Stevens, back around 1851. It seems that Mr. Stevens then was the first man to cast to American waters with a bamboo fly rod.

Within a very few years there were several excellent makers of fly rods here on our shores. They were now involved with various numbers of strips of bamboo, which when assembled and glued had the desired action. A very slow, soft action by our modern standards.

Great names in the history of American tackle had their start in those days—names like Charles Orvis, E. A. Green and Charles Murphy. The Orvis Company is still one of America's fine prestige houses and continues to turn out excellent bamboo fly rods that require the skill and patience of dedicated know-how. Large general tackle companies such as Horrocks-Ibbotson of Utica, N. Y., have been on the American scene for well over 100 years. By 1870, H. L. Leonard of Bangor, Me., was producing his still famous line of six strip bamboo rods for the angling public.

From here on it was one development after another, both in rod making and in reel and line improvements. Bait-casting made great strides again due to better tackle and a continual gain in interest on the part of our sportsmen. But, no matter how you evaluate it, there were still just two types of tackle available—fly rod or bait-casting. The spinning rig, on our shores, was still a long way off!

It would seem that the best outdoor writers of the period before World War I, at least in the field of angling, were researchers, historians, and in several cases, prophets. Prophets most certainly, when we evaluate the works of men such as Emlyn Gill, George LaBranche and Edward R. Hewitt. Their observations and theories, compiled at a time when few were in agreement with them, live on as a monument to their love of angling.

There are many names that reappear through the mists of time—names that are a part of a heritage very dear to the serious fly-fisherman of today. Theodore Gordon and the first dry-fly cast on the waters of New York's Beaverkill—the result of Gordon's correspondence with H. M. Halford and G. E. M. Skues, of England, on this subject of the dry fly. When you consider how few anglers even knew of the dry fly in the early 1900's, it is wonderful indeed that individual dedication was solely responsible for pertinent research on our American waters.

It has been the tedious, patient entomological studies of men like Gordon, Gill, Hewitt, LaBranche, Jennings and Wetzel that have brought fly-fishing to its present degree of acceptance. Without their devotion to the sport, most of us would still be groping in the dark!

Prior to World War II, this writer spent most of his free time, away from school, wading the streams and rivers of New York, New Hampshire and Maine—and occasionally Pennsylvania. It was a time of life when spring meant trout and late summer meant off to the shore for salt water fishing, based at our summer home on the Jersey coast.

Largemouth bass beckoned while bluefish were starting to move close to the jetties and stripers were feeding along the surf, especially during the early hours before dawn. The decisions that had to be made were, I was certain, earth-shattering. The lily-pad ponds and ol' funnelmouth on a bait-casting rig, or Stripers before dawn. Occasionally, my great love of the Beaverkill and the East and West Branch of the Delaware would trouble me and I'd make the long haul up to the

The experts sometimes hate to admit it but there are times when nature's more basic offerings take as many fish as a tackle box full of expensive lures.

The skilled fly-tyer has helped make fly fishing the artful sport it is today. The art is really quite simple to master because of modern equipment and materials.

When you want fishing simplified, free of mechanical problems—look to the young 'uns. They are not complicated by all the reasons of why fish are difficult to catch.

There is a place and a time for each type of tackle. These clear mountain lakes are perfect for ultra-light spinning.

mountains again to see if that old brown trout was still feeding at the jaws of the Beaverkill and East Branch. World War II solved all my problems of indecision! Sharks on a hand line —barracuda in the South Pacific—these were the best we could manage for quite a long spell.

If this angler had ever complained about too many fishermen along the river before the war, he had quite a shock coming within a few years of war's end!

Things were afoot, in Europe, that were to have quite an effect on the streams, rivers and lakes of America. And, quite an effect on the number of anglers that were to look to fishing as a new and exciting recreation. It was the spinning reel. "Lancer leger" means light casting, in the language of the French. Call it what you wish, threadline or fixed-spool—it's all spinning in one form or another, here in America!

To say that spinning enjoys popularity in this country today is like saying that children generally like ice cream. Most of our nation's anglers own a spinning outfit, fish with one and wouldn't be without it. When first introduced in the late '40's, it caught on like wildfire among those new to the world of fishing.

It was found that almost anyone could learn to cast with a spinning reel and rod in about thirty minutes. At least, well enough to be able to go out on a piece of water—tie on a shiny lure, cast and be fast to a started fish that was as surprised as most of the inexperienced anglers. By 1956 it looked as though the "coffee grinders," as they were often called, would take over completely. Fortunately they have not and will not!

Like any method of fishing, spinning has a definite place in the scheme of things. A place where ease of handling, fine light line, and delicate lures must be used and manipulated with finesse. The vast majority of anglers own and use a spinning outfit, but it is a certainty, that the more advanced, knowledgeable group has swung back to a realization that it is no more than a valuable tool among other valuable tools.

The larger bass plugs used in the backwaters of the South, the heavier jigs used in the TVA, or heavy white water areas, and the weed-choked maze of many Muskie lakes call for a bait-casting outfit. Bass-bugging with a fly rod is still the wonderful sport it was before the advent of spinning. And, trout and salmon will always be, traditionally, fly rod fish. Not because anyone insists on this usage but simply because it is more fun on a fly rod and more satisfying sport to most of us.

Each type of tackle, each lure, has a place in the vast network of modern angling as it exists today.

The wise outdoorsman will study the use of all methods and then, with practice, come to use each with skill at the correct time and in the proper place.

The world of fresh water fishing is a fascinating one! It is a world of never-ending surprises, of never completely learned lessons, and, most of all, it is a never ending phantasmagoria of excitement, beauty and nature at its very best!

Now it's time for you to read on and enjoy the world of angling with Messrs. Ovington, McNally, Rosko, Gresham and Seville, with a word or two about trout and salmon by yours truly, Bob Zwirz.

One last word: Look forward to your hours spent on the water as moments well spent in a world that has become a little too frantic, a little too preoccupied with dangerous nonsense. Stand knee deep along the swirling boulder-strewn course of the lovely Beaverkill and close your eyes for just a moment! Relax, and think back to the days of Gordon, of the streamside comradeship of Hewitt and LaBranche, and the contentment it brought to their lives. Remember them, nod to the past and take up where they left this heritage . . . to you.

The fly-rod provides thrills and excitement on our nation's streams and rivers. It is a perfect choice when angling for trout.

CHAPTER II

TROUT AND THE ATLANTIC SALMON

By Bob Zwirz

Trout—Throughout the United States there are, actually, great white water rivers holding fine, healthy trout that are going begging!

Choosing the right place to fish is every bit as important as choosing the right lure. But, it seems to be the same old story —most anglers look for the easy ones and never bother to find the all-important answers that will automatically extend the range of their fishable waters.

We have no intention of suggesting that you wade the canyon run of the Colorado River but we would like to have you open your eyes and examine available trout waters in your state. The reason that we know you were not on the big rainbow stretches of the Androscoggin this summer, while the May flies floated through the turbulent stretches and dace darted along the shore lines, is simple to explain. Three of us fished the white water on this river in New Hampshire for eleven days. We fished the moose in Maine for six and several more equally beautiful streams across the country for a total of forty-seven. You were not fishing in these stretches and, for that matter, neither were your friends. Because at no time did we bump into a single fly fisherman or a single spin fisherman that actually cast a lure to these fast, hissing rapids. We caught some darn big fish. Where were you?

We think we have a pretty good idea just where you were.

You were doing just what we had always done for many, many years. And as summer came with its heat and too numerous fishermen, you sweated it out shoulder to shoulder and settled for the put and take six to nine inch fish that many conservation departments foolishly feel is the only answer. Maybe in some ways this is mostly your own fault. If you don't look for other, more rugged answers, then very possibly you deserve just what you are getting.

19

This writer is going to suggest where you can take fish over 10 inches. You'll get them from those tougher areas while the rest of the boys are griping about the mess the rivers are in.

It is not surprising that between fishing articles, gun articles, travel and a book every once in awhile, this editor gets to spend a great deal of time in the outdoors. While he is going about the business of collecting story material and pictures, he has a fine opportunity to observe his fellow sportsmen.

All too often he finds them in clusters around the bridges and areas nearest the roads. If the truck has been around recently enough, the average sport goes home with several hatchery-raised trout that have all the get-up-and-go of a soggy dish rag. A ten-inch fish is considered "the big one"!

Well, I'm not satisfied with a ten-inch fish from a truck and I'm happy to say that numbered among my close angling friends are several who don't buy this as their criterion of trout fishing either.

This picture of something for nothing has spread from the fishing scene right into hunting. Seems like the same bunch—just wearing different costumes. The road walkers or, even worse, the road riders, looking for their deer. The grouse hunter who seems to forget that it is an upland bird and it takes hard walking and good shooting to collect, and that you have to get some mud on your boots if you are about to locate a flight of woodcock in an alder swamp.

Thinking back before World War II, we can remember being able to walk a couple of hundred feet into the famous Beaverkill, unlimber a fly rod within sight of the car, and walk out three hours later with a threadbare Cahill after releasing 15 to 20 trout, anywhere from 1 to 3 of them going 20 or more. A fond memory!

President Kennedy has sponsored the idea of a physical fitness program for the nation. Tests and records show we need it. This writer is all in favor of a change in mental attitude among our so-called outdoorsmen. Badger your conservation departments; don't settle for sloppy half-hearted programs that improve nothing, that simply kid you into thinking they were doing you a favor by the planting of a few undersized fish, when the truth of the matter is that it takes stream improvement, sensible limit laws, "fishing for sport" stretches and an intelligent concept of just what sport fishing really adds up to.

One more example and I'm through with speech making.

There is a famous river in a very wealthy state that is capable of supporting the fly addict, spin fisherman and even a bait slinger if need be. For many, it has been a river of continual promise and for almost a man's lifetime it has been a great brown trout river. Temperatures have made it too risky for anything but the brown trout once it gets to be August. But year after year it has produced big fish for the serious angler and because of its many tributaries it has had great hold-over and a healthy number of new natives each season.

Last year the N. Y. State Conservation boys announced that from now on streams would receive no brown as they were too difficult to catch. From now on they would stock brook trout. They turned out to be tops, nine inches! But here is the point—the temperature and aeration that a brown has tolerated is too hot for brookies! Their argument is a lulu! They claim that fishermen would rather be able to consistently catch a mess of hatchery Brookies than look like a "loser" with the brown. When reminded of no hold-over and the temperature problem, they shrugged it off with a curt "Most of them will be caught by then, anyway." That is the kind of long range planning you're getting for your tax dollar. What kind of prima donnas are the outdoor bunch turning into when they allow themselves to be treated or thought of with this watered down kind of hogwash for a program?

I spoke, earlier, about a little known or accepted river in New Hampshire, the Androscoggin. It is good only in an area between Berlin and Errol in the northern tip of the state. Eventually, when the taxpayer wises up, it may be free of pollution, logs and problems for the remainder of its many miles. But that long, fabulous stretch of winding, roaring water is enough to calm spirits. Starting from the dam in Errol you can look forward to landlocked salmon, rainbows, brookies and heaven knows what else. I've watched men stare at the great boiling runs and salmon-like pools that whirl and surge like dark ink over hundreds of boulders . . . stare, and shrug, and get back into their cars and take off for some crowded ankle-deep stream with its promise of a recent hatchery truck delivery.

We talked to the local boys and to Paul Mathieu, local conservation officer based in Errol. Paul, who is a crack outdoorsman, a fine sportsman and the best walking public relations man I've yet to meet, confirmed our thinking about the river. He told us of the mixed bag and the size fish that

The Rangely Lakes area of Maine provide great fishing for trout, and land-locked salmon. Here is a trophy that will bring the angler back again, next year.

were taken by those who learned the river's quirks and secrets, rainbows to 5 pounds, brookies to 4, and landlocks to near 7.

We decided one of us would fish wets and streamers, one spin and the other fish live bait in the big holes. From the high oxygen pockets of the many series of rapids we caught hold-over rainbows, none under 12 inches. Several up to 17! Brookies made the grade and two, of more than 70 we caught, went to 3¼ pounds. Some of the big runs took skillful wading and accurate casting. On more than one occasion one or the other would be soaked by a spill in the heavier stretches. Many likely spots just couldn't be reached by a lure without a helicopter but in this "unfishable" river we pulled out the stops, thanks to the direction of Paul Mathieu.

The day before we left two things happened that might interest you. When it comes to imagination here is what I mean.

Three local men pulled a car-top boat down a steep, difficult slope and then went back and returned with a couple of live bait buckets. Then they manipulated that boat out into the roaring mass of water, worked it above a turbulent pool that is easily 400 feet wide and 600 long. They fished with baitcasting tackle, sinkers and small bullheads; one fished a gob of big worms. They bounced these along the bottom time and time again, each time covering more pool. They took fish that you would think impossible. The largest Rainbow was five ounces under five pounds and it was a gorgeous specimen. "Does anyone else do this?" I asked. "No!" was the answer. They had never seen anyone above that pool.

Second lesson began as conversation, a bet and a dare—a little foolish I'll admit. There was a terrific looking eddy on the other side of the river in an area where there was no road. We watched a substantial trout rise several times for May flies, just where an eddy joined with fast white water. Couldn't reach it with a cast and had no boat with us. And then it dawned on me. I remembered the Marines and my lessons, took off my khaki trousers, tied each cuff into a knot, walked a quarter of a mile above the spot, filled the pants with air as they hit the water, grabbed the rod and floated down to the head of the eddy like a rocket. It took two casts. The trout weighed 3 pounds 10 ounces! It not only gave me a fine fish but gave us all a good laugh that night over dinner.

It was the same on the Moose River in Maine, only tougher

to wade, if possible, at least on the far off white water stretches we located. Again the salmon, the big trout and always the hard, hard routine. Nothing easy, but then, nothing small.

It has been the same out west on the Snake River and on many others we can remember. Turbulent bully-boy stretches that nobody seems to love if you can judge it by the number of anglers you meet. Not a soul, not a hatchery truck—just big fish waiting for you.

Look around your state. Find the alder-choked streams where big solitary browns live, untouched year after year. Find the white, tricky runs that people say don't hold fish and study the pockets and the eddies, and break off on a five-pounder that is king in his foaming, hissing maelstrom. Come back again another day and try him again. His kind is always there in those dangerous spots.

The only trouble so far, as I see it, is that *you* haven't been!

Technique for trout fishing is a varied proposition, most difficult to detail in such a small book. We can, however, give you the basics of tackle use and fundamental ways of catching trout that will give you the most pleasure.

Brown, brook and rainbow trout are caught in creeks, small brooks, large, fast-flowing rivers and lakes in the northern belt of states, Canada and Alaska. While the smaller of the trout are basically insect eaters, they soon grow to a size when bait fish or small fish of their own species become their prey.

The imitations of the insects are made of fur, feathers, yarn, tinsel and a variety of other materials which are tied to a hook and are called flies. Dry flies, imitations of the stream bred cadis, May flies and stone flies are tied to represent these specific insects that hatch on the surface of the lakes and streams. Wet flies are tied to represent the drowned insects that either float on or near the surface of the water. The nymph patterns are tied specifically to approximate the underwater stage of aquatic insect development. Streamer and bucktail flies are tied to represent stream minnows.

All of these plus worms and live minnows can be cast with a long, slender fly rod with the reel mounted behind the handle. Tapered lines and leaders are designed to fit the action, weight and length of the rod so that the entire outfit casts the specific lure easiest and farthest toward its destination, in the current or on the placid surface of a pool or section of the lake.

Fast-water fishing for Rainbows is a test of skills and balance. Here is a fine Beaverkill trout taken during the early spring high water.

Spinning gear is designed to cast spinning lures, spinners, spoons, and a myriad of underwater lures heavier than the flies, and, of course, bait that is either alive or dead. This tackle is designed light for small trout and stream fishing where neither the fish nor the lures are too large. Heavier spinning rods and reels are made for bigger game as well. This tackle can be used for casting small lures, trolling rigs deep down or bait fishing.

While bait casting rods and reels with the multiplying spools can be used for trout fishing, they are most generally used for bass, pike and musky fishing, as the lures used are generally larger. It is quite impossible to cast tiny metal lures or flies with a bait casting outfit.

Stream fishing for trout demands that the angler work the currents where the fish are lying, if there is not a feeding period obviously present. Trout generally lie at the heads of pools, behind rocks and snags, or well down at the tail of the pool in the shallows. When they begin to feed, they work into the avenues of current that carry the food to them.

Lake fishing usually demands the technique of trolling, or, if fish are seen to be rising to insects or chasing bait fish, or casting to them with either spinning tackle or fly rod gear.

To be properly equipped, the trout fisherman, having yet to establish a preference, should have a good trout fly rod of from seven to eight feet in length with a line to balance and a single action fly reel to hold the line. Tapered leaders from seven to nine feet are tied in between the line and the fly so the lure can be delivered to the fish without the line scaring the trout. A large selection of all types of flies should be in the tackle box.

Spinning gear should be light or medium and with monofilament nylon to match. Lures from tiny spinners to the larger spoons and revolving types should be in the collection.

Bait fishing demands sinkers and hooks, and of course a healthy supply of lively worms, or minnows that are kept alive at least until they are placed on the hook.

It is best to get to know the waters you will be fishing generally and also to know their pattern from the beginning of the season to the end, so that you can adapt your techniques and tackle to the situation of the moment. This is delightful to learn. If you are traveling to strange country it is best to visit the local tackle store and also, if a guide or local citizen can take you in hand, to follow his advice.

Learn to watch the successful fishermen on the stream or

Trout and the Atlantic Salmon

27

lake. Copy their techniques and note the lures they are using.

The fisherman intending to wade the stream or lake to do his trout fishing should have a pair of light weight boots, not the fireman kind! They should have well cleated soles. For deeper wading, a pair of rubberized waders reaching to the chest are recommended. In fact, waders are preferred over boots, since most of us like to wade as deep as possible. For many years we have been thankful that we have had the extra margin in order to wade deep enough.

Both waders and boots should be equipped with chains for gravel bottoms and felt soles for the slippery rocks or moss-covered stones and rocks.

The fisherman should also have a fishing vest to wear over his regular clothes. This has a lot of pockets. Vests like the Lee Wulff Tackle-Pak also have snaps to hold your rod while changing lures and a strap to which your landing net is attached. Your whole outfit, camera, fly and lure boxes, leader boxes, fly dope, matches, cigarettes, license, wallet, etc., etc. can be stored safely. There is also an attached creel on some models.

Of course every picturesque fisherman wears a hat, though not necessarily an old smelly one. A real fishing hat has a hatband into which you can stick used flies. It also acts to ward off the direct sunlight.

Other than a wading staff, if you are going in for rough fast-water fishing, and if you intend to keep your fish, a landing net specially made for wading (short handle) and a creel to keep your catch complete the Waltonian costume.

Salmon—In northern New England it is often referred to as "Kennebec." Whatever name it may be known by, the Atlantic salmon of our continent and the coast of Europe is the true prince of fly rod angling.

Probably more money is spent, per salmon caught, than on any other species. When we thoroughly analyze costs of travel, lodging, equipment and in many cases guides, it becomes a pretty stiff tariff for men of average means. However, once the angler gets his first taste of this sport and connects with a good fish, he is hooked for life.

I've talked to many anglers before they took off on that first salmon trip. They did not seem too upset about the cost of that new salmon rod, nor were they particularly bothered by the cost of salmon flies, line and leaders. But believe me, many were bothered by the need to pay for a guide along with all the other expenses.

Minnow-like lures account for a good proportion of large trout. This lure works deep where the big ones take cover.

For the man new to salmon and their habits, and for that matter a stranger to the river he plans to fish, nothing could handicap him more than trying to operate without a guide. Until you realize that an Atlantic salmon has few of the needs, while in the river, of say brown trout, you will surely fish him incorrectly. First, consider the fact that salmon station themselves for relative comfort in the flow, not in a typical trout feeding station. If you are a complete novice, it will be difficult for you to accept the single truth that salmon do not feed while involved in their upstream battle to the spawning areas.

Next, let's consider the art of knowing one's river. The guide that will accompany you and advise you is almost surely a native of the region and, better yet, a devotee of this particular river. He has learned through the years just where the salmon will lie, and just as important to you, how to cast to it.

There will not be space enough for me to write with any thoroughness concerning methods, tricks and the like to take the Atlantic salmon. For the most part, we will discuss places to consider if you are about to plan your first trip. There will be but a suggestion as to actual methods.

The first intelligent act of any novice in planning his trip should be, in my estimate, to beg, borrow or steal a copy of Lee Wulff's excellent book "The Atlantic Salmon." It has every conceivable bit of salmon lore within its pages that you will require.

Top patterns in traditional wet flies: (average sizes: #4, #6, #8). Dusty Miller, Black Dose, Jock Scott, Mar Lodge and Silver Grey. Add to these a few of the top recommended guides' patterns. Hook size will depend on stream and weather conditions and can call for small, low water patterns. Or, right down to 3/0's for visibility under certain circumstances.

Top dry fly patterns: The Wulff patterns, Rat-faced Mc-Dougall, Whiskers, fished in the style of a skater, and a new favorite of mine—again designed by my friend Lee Wulff— the plastic-bodied surface Stone Fly. Hook size will vary according to conditions and specific pattern chosen.

Since the Atlantic salmon is built to jump high water falls, and to migrate up miles of fast-water streams, and since he has learned to grow big and fat and strong in the ocean, he is no cinch to kill with anything but proper tackle.

Salmon fishing is limited in this country and Canada to the use of the fly rod. This means that the rod must be able to conquer this jumper of the wilds. Sometimes you will see salmon upwards of 40 pounds coming to your fly. If you are not equipped to whip him, he will whip you!

While many of the more expert salmon fishermen can break any big fish with a medium to heavy regulation eight-foot fly rod usually used for trout and fly rod bass fishing, it is strongly recommended that you use a longer rod with a more powerful taper. It is not only the power of the fight that you need, but often it is absolutely necessary to cast a long distance and generally into a pesky wind that somehow seems to blow right at you.

With this staunch rod, a tapered line to balance the action and weight of the rod is needed to get that line out there with a minimum of hard work. A long, tapered monofilament leader is next and then comes the fly.

The salmon reel must have a large capacity and be strongly built. Usually the 35- or 45-yard tapered line is backed by at least 100 yards of 15-pound test level bait casting line. When salmon take off for parts unknown and you do not have a backing there to hold them, you'll be busted up, very likely on the first run. Many times a salmon will run you out of all your backing as he heads up or down stream. When the backing gets low, you take after him by wading the stream or running along the bank.

Salmon do not fool around. They don't teach you the tricks of the trade by degrees. They "learn you" almost at once.

There is a lot of luck in salmon fishing. First of all, you have to be there at the right time, when they are there. The water level has to be just right or they won't pay any attention to your flies. Some anglers have been traveling many miles every year to catch their first salmon. Others are lucky enough to connect first time out. All agree that the right gear is needed even with the hoped-for luck.

Where To Go For Your Atlantic Salmon: (Fly rod only, of course.)

Labrador—is still far from being easily accessible. Accommodations are scarce and guides not readily available. Float planes are the best bet and you will be happy to note that there are no leased or restricted waters. A non-resident fishing license puts you, legally, on any river.

Best bets: The Eagle River (south Labrador), the Forteau (southern Labrador) and the Adlatok near Hopedale. Be prepared to rough it if you choose the relatively unfinished area of Labrador.

Newfoundland: If you are a thorough planner, you can find excellent fishing in the following: The Humber River or Portland Creek. Guides are mandatory in Newfoundland.

Nova Scotia: Public fishing and no closed water. My favorite here is the northwest Margaree, one of the most beautiful salmon streams I've fished to date. It is definitely a "late" river. I prefer the three weeks before October 15th closing. Next we have the Medway, south of Halifax, and the St. Mary's River, a flow of considerable size. Guides are not mandatory unless fishing in a heavily wooded area.

Quebec: It is advisable to know exactly where you are going when you plan a trip to the Province of Quebec. Excellent accommodations are to be had, a complete list of all facilities are available from the Department of Fish and Game for the province. At this time there are only a few rivers that are open to public angling. Among them we have the Matane, the Little Cascapedia and the Romaine. The vast remainder are under lease and require that you be a guest at some establishment or of a private individual who has angling rights.

Two of this continent's finest salmon rivers are within the confines of this province. They are the Moise and the Natashquan. Consider also the Gaspé river area, the Matapedia and the Grand Cascapedia. The Port Daniel River on the Gaspé, just east of the Little Cascapedia, offers some water operated by the government at nominal angling costs.

My choice for an inexpensive salmon trip for the uninitiated would be to try the twenty-five miles of the Matane. There is good food and lodging in the local town of Matane.

New Brunswick: It's impossible to talk Atlantic Salmon without mentioning the famed Miramichi River chain. It's still one of the greatest producers of salmon in the world. It is not surprising to find that most of the water is leased. It is, of course, available to you if you are a guest or staying at one of the many fishing camps that populate New Brunswick as well as this famed river.

Many anglers are becoming interested in the so-called "black" salmon fishing of spring. It is a somewhat inferior form of salmon fishing in the estimate of this writer-angler, but is still on the increase. As these are a "spent" fish that have wintered on the hard side, it should be obvious that these will not be the great game fish that started up-river the previous summer. Complete brochures and information are available without cost from the New Brunswick Travel Bureau, Fredericton, New Brunswick, Canada.

Maine: Due to the work of ·a dedicated few, it is now possible to say that some Maine rivers are making a come-back. Chemical wastes and dams are still the great problem but, little by little, progress is in the making. This past season I had the opportunity to spend several days in Maine and took the time to check river conditions and talk to a few local anglers about the salmon's return.

This "return" is far from satisfactory at this writing but it is definitely improving year by year. If you are planning a trip to this state and you are of a pioneering nature it might well be to your advantage to take a salmon rod along.

At this writing there are several rivers listed as containing salmon. It is this writer's opinion that you will fare best on either the Narraguagus, Machias or the Dennys. For the time being, the Penobscot and Aroostook rivers are too large for the visiting angler to stumble on the relatively few fish that are moving up.

How would you like to kill a salmon like this British Columbia tyee taken by this happy angler? When these fish are running, they are no more difficult to spot than any school fish. Being able to handle one on even the heavy gear is something else again.

CHAPTER III

STEELHEAD AND PACIFIC SALMON ANGLING

By Ray Ovington

From the ice encrusted flows of Alaska to the palm tree country of Central California, the cutthroat steelhead trout and the various species of Pacific Salmon reign supreme as food and game fishes.

Western residents and those wise to the quick transportation by air from the East are blessed with both species of fish that have all the qualities of the gamey Atlantic salmon without the Eastern restrictions of where to go, season limitation or posted water.

Arguments as to which is the gamier fish have long since been settled. Anglers limited to either species hold theirs as the gamiest. Time was when large Atlantic salmon over the 15-pound mark were common catches in Maine, New Brunswick and other Eastern Canadian waters. These fish, being larger than the average steelhead obviously gave more of a fight, even though both species are known for their tremendous power and high jumps, but Atlantic salmon sizes have declined while the steelhead has remained the same, equalizing the picture.

Both fish have one thing in common. They are andronomous, that is, they spend most of their life in the ocean, growing big and strong on marine life. When the urge to spawn comes, they ascend the rivers of this vast coastline to the farthest reaches of the snow capped mountains, fighting against strong currents, high waterfalls and ruinous rough waters. The Pacific salmon also ascends the rivers for the same reasons.

The Pacific salmon, and we are concerned here with the chinook and the silver, differs from the Atlantic in that it ascends the streams only once, dying after the spawning action. The Atlantic can ascend as many as five times, growing bigger with each sojourn in the brine.

Why did nature arrange things this way? Simple. There are fewer rivers on the Atlantic coast than there are on the Pacific. At least that is a non-scientific reasonable answer. If the Pacific salmon were allowed to ascend more than once the rivers would be overrun. As it is, the streams are choked with these finny migrants and rivers are actually clogged with them at the peak of their run.

There is no season of the year when you cannot find a run of salmon or steelhead somewhere on the West Coast. This does not mean, however, that finding a pool full of fish is as easy as one might imagine.

For steelhead and cutthroat trout the two basic seasons when the rivers become alive are winter, from December to April, and summer, from May to September.

The king salmon or chinooks come to the rivers from June through September and run from 20 to 75 pounds in weight. Young kings of smaller size are called blackmouths. The silver or cohoes enter the same waters about a month later and are found there as late as November, sometimes lingering on into December.

Any migrating fish is unpredictable. They can move many miles in one night. You might be fishing a pool loaded with fish one day and not see a sign of anything larger than a minnow for the next week until another school arrives on the scene.

Generally speaking, the salmon ascend the stream first, followed by the steelhead and cutthroat trout, subspecies of the rainbow. These second placers follow the salmon for a very good reason. They feed on the eggs which do not settle in the beds where they have been laid. When this condition is prevalent, single salmon eggs or imitations of same are the lures to use with a fly rod or light spinning rod. While steelhead do take flies, particularly after they have been back in their birthplace home of the fresh water, they revert, as the Atlantic salmon do, to feeding on flies and insects, and occasionally will take a minnow imitation tied in the typical style of large wet flies that resemble the eastern streamer and bucktail flies used in conventional eastern trout and landlocked salmon fishing.

Most of the best salmon angling is not in the upper reaches of the mountain streams, but is found in abundance at the mouths and estuaries of rivers. Here the anglers gang up by anchoring their boats side by side in the current, and instead of trolling merely allow their shiny minnow imitation and herring imitation lures to wobble in the current downstream from their anchorage. Steelhead trout are also caught this way, though most sportsmen prefer to catch them in the conventional way of bait cast with spinning gear, lures spincast or single eggs, artificial lures or flies worked from the fly rod.

Some of the best salmon action is had by trolling in the salt water near the inlets of rivers much the same way the Easterner fishes for striped bass. As a matter of fact, quite often the salmon troller will pick up stripers as far south as San Francisco and as far north as Victoria Island, British Columbia, right along with the salmon.

With such a choice of fish, the various species of salmon, and the steelhead to choose from and the enormous amount of area in which to fish, it is a difficult task to pin down any specific area or time of the year where we could safely say that you would be likely to hit into a good batch of fish.

There is a general routine, however, which can be used as a guide.

If you cannot make up your mind as to which state you will concentrate on for your fishing, write to all of the West Coast fish and game departments, listed at the back of this book. Ask about seasons, times of the year, general current conditions and their prognostications which are based on past migrations of these fish. By doing this you can put together the pieces of the picture puzzle and arrive at a routine for your travels from south to north or vice versa. This would make a marvelous excursion for the entire family, for there is much to see, at least in California, Oregon and Washington, even if your time or limitations forbid crossing the border into British Columbia.

Many of the principal cities along the coast have their salmon derbies and fishing contests. They have learned by experience just when the peak of the fish will be running. Take your cue from these dates.

While it is not always a desirable idea to follow the crowd, it is a necessary evil in the case of these fish. Fortunately there are enough streams to go around and most of the popular rivers are large and broad to accommodate many anglers in the hot spots. There are also many and varied kinds of transportation, guide services and boat rentals where you can set up headquarters and also get the information as to the current runs of fish, and what they are taking them on.

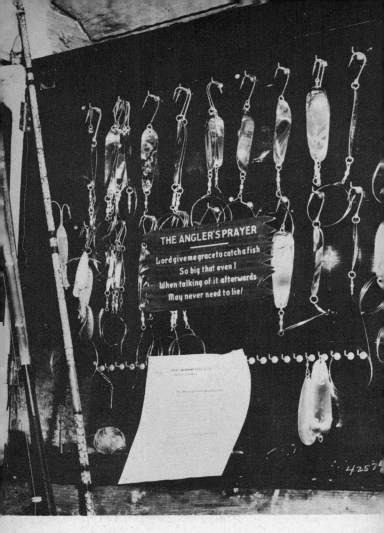

THE ANGLER'S PRAYER

Lord give me grace to catch a fish
So big that even I
When talking of it afterwards
May never need to lie!

A variety of shining lures and spoons make up the typical
lures which are trolled and cast for the biggest salmon. While
these fish are still in the ocean or in the inlets, they will take
such hardware. Rarely are they ever taken on fly fishermen's
lures upstream.

A fine specimen of a heavy sea run rainbow from the Skagit River, State of Washington. Taken on light spinning gear, this monster gave the angler quite a battle for many exciting minutes.

Lower Arrow Lake on the Columbia River, British Columbia, Canada. Many Americans cross into Canada by launch, heading north to the two Arrow Lakes in the Rockies. All trout and steelhead are found in such waters.

If you like the idea, you can enter a local derby and compete with the best of the talent, remembering that these ocean-going gamesters are no respecter of persons.

As to tackle specifications, take along your medium or stout spinning rod for ocean trolling or for winter steelhead stream fishing. You will troll heavy lures and cast heavy globs of eggs for this season. In the spring and summer, single eggs cast on a tiny single hook weighted for the current can be handled with the spinning rod or even the fly rod. Artificial lures such as spoons and spinners can be cast with the conventional spincasting rod and reel.

Those who prefer to use bait casting reels will need a longer tipped rod than the conventional bass fishing rod of four or five feet, although the usual bass rod will be all right for trolling and very short casting work.

The fly fisherman working the steelhead rivers can use the same rod that he would use for Atlantic salmon or bass bug fishing. In some of the smaller streams he could even get away with the conventional shorter length fly rod used for one- and two-pound fish of the typical eastern stream size. His fly reels should be of a large capacity for ample backing, say, at least 50 yards or more behind his tapered line that is balanced to the rod for long casts into the wind.

Terminal tackle includes tapered leaders whether he use the single hook and salmon egg or the artificial fly.

As far as the selection of lures and flies is concerned, the many fishing books and also the recommendations of the lure manufacturers can be used as a guide, but guide only. As usual, when you are limited to a short fishing trip and are working strange waters it is far better and a time saver to inquire from the local tackle shop, local chamber of commerce or, if you are lucky, a good friend, in order to find out the pattern or technique of the moment in any given stretch of water, or for that matter any specific stream.

If you have never caught anything over the size of a hatchery brook trout, or possibly nothing more fighty than a pesky smallmouth bass, you are in for some potent surprises when you hit into your first steelhead. Even the seasoned Atlantic salmon fisherman can be shown up as a duffer by these fast running monsters.

Not only do these fish jump and jump, perhaps as many as ten times, but they also can make desperate runs of as much as fifty yards at a clip. You have to keep your rod high so as not to have the line fouled on underwater obstructions, but you might even have to try running along the shore line to keep up with a fish that is bound to return to the ocean.

Remember that any fish that has the strength to migrate up hazardous and constantly killing type water is built to take both it and the pressure of your rod.

Don't try to horse in a good-sized steelhead, or your tackle will end up as kindling wood.

Same goes for the salmon, particularly when they are taken in the open ocean. The eastern striped bass man used to fishing the surf or trolling the estuaries seldom has the treatment dealt him that even a medium-sized Pacific salmon can dole out. Their runs are long and speedy and they will often sound down deep for quite a spell, only to change their mind in lightning speed to dance for a while on the surface. It takes a cool hand and lots of luck to hold tight enough, yet not risk breaking the fish off.

A string of largemouth black bass caught on Zwirz's Marabou Eel by angler Don Bingler.

CHAPTER IV

BASS, PIKE, AND MUSKELLUNGE FISHING

By Tom McNally

Excluding the trouts, black bass, northern pike and muskellunge comprise the "big three" of the fresh water game fish family. For millions of American anglers, bass, pike, and muskies are synonymous with fresh water fishing. The bass is nothing more than a lip with fins; the nothern is a needle-nosed gangster; and the muskellunge is a tough-skinned roustabout whose perpetual expression is a sneer. Individually or grouped, members of the "big three" clan likely provide more fresh water excitement than all the other inland fish species combined.

The largemouth black bass is the most sought—and found —fresh water game fish in America. It is the most widely distributed, appearing in every state in the continental United States excepting Alaska. In fully half the states, it is the most abundant and popular fresh water game fish. Fishing for bass in many areas is a year-round proposition, and in a majority of the states angling restrictions covering bass are limited.

Bass are members of the sunfish family, and are considered a "warm water" species. There are several kinds of bass now recognized by ichthyologists; the largemouth black bass, the Florida largemouth black bass, the smallmouth black bass, the spotted bass, the Suwannee bass, and the redeye bass. Most fishermen generally classify bass as either "largemouth" or "smallmouth" and, practically speaking, this division is adequate.

The Florida largemouth, the Suwannee, and the spotted bass (also called Kentucky bass) are comparatively restricted in range, and the redeye bass is really just another kind of smallmouth bass.

All of the basses may appear in either lakes or rivers. The largemouth, however, is primarily a lake or pond fish, while the smallmouth will thrive in clear, fast-flowing rivers as well as in clean, cold northern lakes. In many places both large mouth and small mouth bass are coexistent, but normally one species will dominate. Generally speaking, the largemouth is a southern fish—doing best in the warm waters of the Southland—while the smallmouth prefers the cool waters of the northern states. The greatest overlapping of the two species is in the TVA lakes, the big mid-America impoundments such as Kentucky Lake, Lake Cumberland, Dale Hollow, and Bull Shoals Reservoir.

The largemouth is much more adaptable than the smallmouth. He may be as much at home in a north Wisconsin lake as he would be in a south Louisiana bayou. On the other hand, the smallmouth has well-defined likes and dislikes—and if the water and the temperature and the food supply are not exactly to his taste he will not survive, or at least will not prosper.

I have had excellent largemouth bass fishing in a small lake in southern Ontario—smack in the middle of Canada's world-famed smallmouth belt, but this was the exception to the rule that most largemouths have a southern drawl. Florida's bass fishing is, of course, justly famous. Although largemouths of more than ten pounds are not taken there with the regularity that chambers-of-commerce would like you to believe, some bass in the fifteen-pound class are taken in Florida waters annually. Some of the state's lesser-known spots—such as the Withlacoochee River and Orange Lake—frequently give up exceptional trophy bass.

The tiny ponds on the lower eastern shore of Maryland, and in Virginia, often provide very fast largemouth fishing. But throughout the country there are similar spots where, when things are right, it appears a largemouth is lurking beneath every lily pad.

Among the best-known largemouth waters are the TVA lakes, Florida's St. John's River and Lake Okeechobee, Lake Mead on the Nevada-Arizona border, and the brackish waters of Chesapeake Bay in Maryland and Virginia, and of Albemarle and Pamlico Sounds in North Carolina.

Famed waters for smallmouth bass include Basswood Lake and others in the Minnesota-Ontario border lakes country, various ponds in southeastern Maine (such as Skoodic Pond), the Bass Islands area of Lake Erie, northern Lake Michigan, the St. Lawrence River, the Susquehanna and Potomac rivers, and various lakes and rivers in southern Manitoba, Ontario, and Quebec. Lower Ontario smallmouth fishing is extraordinary, and the Winnipeg River in Manitoba offers exceptional small mouth angling.

There are as many different ways to catch black bass as
there are fishermen. They are caught by still-fishing with
live bait, by spinning, plug casting, fly fishing, and trolling.
Which tackle is best and which technique is most productive
depends upon the season and the water being fished. The all-
around bass fishing expert will employ all casting methods as
well as trolling, according to the dictates of his experience
and the existing conditions.

Generally speaking, the average bass fisherman errs by
devoting too much time to casting plugs and spoons along
shallow shore lines. Although bass often frequent such areas,
they are found in deep water through most of the fishing season. Also, both largemouth and smallmouth are school fish,
spending more of their time rubbing shoulders with one another than the casual fisherman believes.

It is not possible to digest in limited space the tackle tricks
and angling techniques required to consistently produce bass.
But a thumbnail sketch of bass-busting includes use of fly,
spinning, and bait or plug casting tackle, and also trolling.
Easily the sportiest, and frequently most rewarding, way to
take bass is with the fly rod and conventional bass bugs. I
prefer a nine-foot, five-ounce fly rod with matching GAF
line and frill-less cork bugs tied on 3X long-shank hooks.
Both largemouth and smallmouths are suckers for bugs when
the fish are in the shallows. At such times a large streamer
fly may produce as well, and in clear rivers an orange, white,
or yellow marabout streamer often will belt smallmouths
where it hurts.

If it is discovered bass are too deep to take with the fly rod,
you may get down to them by chucking out spoons or plugs
with spinning or bait casting gear. Use lures of different types
and weights, fish them at varying depths and places until bass
are located. Bottom-bouncing with lead-head jigs having
marabout, bucktail, or polar bear "winging" is a deadly system. The newer plastic or rubber "worms" and "eels," also
fished on bottom, are unusually effective. Too many fishermen nowadays overlook the various pork baits, including
the porkrind "eel," pork "chunk" and pork "frog," as well
as the ordinary porkrind strip. The latter is used primarily
as garnishment for a spoon; while the former are normally
used as individual lures. Fished slowly along bottom, the
black porkrind "eel" is a bass killer. And when Mr. Big-
mouth is in the lilies or the weed beds, a white pork "chunk"

or "frog" hits him like an axe between the eyes.

The northern pike should not be confused with the eastern chain pickerel. These are fish of a similar type, but there the likeness ends. They look alike to some extent, but there's a major difference in size and distribution. Northern pike are found primarily in the northern states, especially in the Midwest states, and from central to southern Canada. The chain pickerel is less abundant, confined primarily to the Lake Ontario drainage, and south and east of the Appalachians. Northerns weighing more than 30 pounds are caught annually, and there is evidence the fish may attain as much as 50 pounds. Chain pickerel, however, rarely exceed five pounds, and more often weigh two to three pounds.

The best northern pike fishing is not in the United States, although Alaska has some good pike fishing. Northern pike are circumpolar in distribution, but in this hemisphere the finest pike angling is in Manitoba, Saskatchewan and Ontario —and probably in that order. All the Canadian provinces have some pike, as do many of the northern states, but giant pike and really fast pike fishing are products of virgin waters. The northern pike, as a rule, is not a difficult fish to take, and as a consequence even top northern pike water can be quickly depleted. It has been my good fortune to have fished in nearly all of the states, and in every Canadian province. In my experience the best pike fishing exists in Manitoba and Saskatchewan.

While certain lakes in the northern states, and lakes in Quebec and Ontario, occasionally provide excellent northern pike fishing, their pike angling normally does not compare favorably to that in Manitoba and Saskatchewan season-to-season. Quebec and Ontario lakes have, for the most part, been exploited by sportsmen for years, and no longer are many of their pike waters difficult to reach. New roads are bridging the wilderness, and some of the last strongholds of trophy-size pike are now crawling with anglers.

Labrador, portions of Alberta, the Northwest Territories, and similar arctic and sub-arctic lands have some excellent pike lakes, but northerns do not prosper in really far northern waters. In general the major "pike belt" lies between the 55th and 60th parellel, although there are, of course, some scattered trophy pike lakes a bit beyond latitude 60.

Minnesota, Wisconsin, Michigan, and North Dakota are the best pike states, and probably in that order. Minnesota has much more suitable pike water than any of the other

Northern pike and largemouth black bass live together in the backwaters of the Mississippi River.

states named. Michigan and North Dakota have the least. Pike ranging from 10 to 20 pounds are caught with regularity in Minnesota, and in somewhat lesser numbers in Wisconsin. All Wisconsin lakes have been fished hard over the years, and while many of them still provide fast pike fishing, in few of them is there much chance of catching a sizable northern.

Almost any angling method will take pike, but bait casting for them is most popular, with spinning running a close second. In areas where pike run heavy, stout bait casting tackle is preferred to spinning gear by the majority of experienced anglers. Trolling accounts for a great number of pike, but if the water being fished has a decent northern concentration, trolling should not be necessary. Trolling is certainly the least sporty way to catch pike, since this fish has a penchant for striking cast lures.

Pike frequent the shallows, and thus are a made-to-order species for the fisherman who prefers to flip-and-reel a lure rather than to sit and troll one. This is not to say that pike will not go deep (I have caught them at depths of 60 feet). But most of the season, in the prime pike range, northerns will be found hovering in weed beds at depths of from one to 15 feet. In June, in Manitoba and Saskatchewan lakes, you will find northerns in less than five feet of water.

The northern is a fiercely predatory fish. In wilderness lakes he often has complete disdain for fishermen, boats, and lures. Once, at Mitchell Lake in Manitoba, I spied a 21-pound northern resting on his fins near the surface, in three feet of water. With a plug casting outfit I tossed a large spoon just beyond the fish's nose. He turned and followed it to the boat. He struck it right under the bow, even though I was in plain sight. The hook pulled out immediately. I twitched the spoon, and the northern struck again. He hit three more times, always within a few feet of the rod tip, before being hooked, boated, weighed and released.

If there is one best lure for northern pike it is a red-and-white spoon. But spoons of any type or finish are good, as are numerous wobbling plugs. The fish will take top water lures, but sparkling underwater lures usually have the edge. Regardless of what lure is used, a very slow retrieve should be maintained. Northerns are agreeable strikers, but they dislike expending the energy necessary to chase a lure.

Northern pike have needle-like canine teeth, and hundreds of close-knit smaller teeth on their lips, palate, and roof of the mouth. A short, light wire leader is desirable, or a shocker length of 20, 30, or 40 pound test nylon. Neither wire nor heavy nylon is necessary if only small northerns are available.

While fly fishing for northern pike is not commonly done, the fish can be readily taken by fly fishing. They will rise to either streamer flies or popping bugs, but they take streamers much more readily than poppers. Where big pike are the rule, streamers measuring five or six inches long should be used. Best colors are red-and-yellow, with yellow predominant, followed by red-and-white. The streamers should be tied on heavy 1/0 to 6/0 hooks, with the hackles tied in splayed-wing style.

In fly-in lakes in Manitoba and Saskatchewan, I have caught numbers of northern pike weighing 10 to 15 pounds on flies. In First Cranberry Lake, Manitoba, I boated an 18-pounder; and at Black Lake, Saskatchewan, an 18½-pounder—both on streamer flies. I have hooked and lost, on flies, still larger northerns—some that likely would have gone to 25 pounds. In fly fishing for pike a 12-inch length of 30- or 40-pound nylon is recommended as a shock tippet.

The muskellunge is the largest fresh water fish an American angler can hope to catch, with the exception of sturgeon and alligator gar. The world record musky, from the St. Lawrence River, weighed 69 pounds, 15 ounces, and others in the 60-pound class have been taken on rod and reel. Each year muskies weighing more than 40 pounds are caught, and ones weighing 20 to 30 pounds are commonplace.

Perhaps no fresh water fish is more frustrating than the musky. It takes a lot of space (it has been estimated by biologists that an adult musky requires no less than four acres of "living room") and considerable time to grow a trophy musky. Thus nowhere are there really very many muskies, and in addition the fish are exceptionally moody. Some days, it seems, anyone on the lake with a rod will experience action of some sort from the muskies; but most of the time even the most dedicated musky hunter will spend days on end casting fruitlessly.

The problem of where to go for a musky is simplified by the distribution of the fish. They're found in some of the Great Lakes states, including Ohio, and to a much lesser extent in West Virginia and Pennsylvania. The St. Lawrence River is a good spot to seek a large muksy, and south Canada has a number of good musky lakes. But northern Wisconsin is the real stronghold of the musky, and has produced most of the world record fish.

Wisconsin has a major hatchery and restocking program that bolsters its musky population. Small muskies, ranging eight to twelve inches, are planted in suitable Wisconsin rivers and lakes annually. This is one instance in which a hatching-stocking program has proved to be valuable on the basis of tag returns from marked fish.

If there is one sure way to catch a musky it is to go where muskies are, and then to cast, cast, cast—and, finally, cast some more. Some long-time musky "experts" purport to have this fishing down "to a science," and doubtlessly there are right and wrong ways to try for muskies, but in this game nothing produces as well as persistence.

Many Wisconsin muskellunge regulars insist all they really do is locate a musky, then try for him day after day until, eventually, the fish hits. However, even a musky strike does not necessarily equal a musky in the boat. The fish are exceptionally hard-mouthed and difficult to hook. Moreover, the musky is nothing like the average northern pike in fighting characteristics. Muskies are powerful, wildly-leaping ruffians, and if you hook a good one you will, normally, have a fight to remember.

Grits Gresham fishing Wyoming beach pond—raising rod tip at end of cast to make fly touch water first.

The multiplying reel where one revolution of the handle means several of the spool—is an American invention.

CHAPTER V

HOW TO USE YOUR TACKLE

By Grits Gresham

Fishing success is almost invariably linked to efficient casting. There are exceptions, of course, such as cane pole fishing or trolling, but with all other types of angling it is most often the guy who can make his gear talk who has something to talk about after the trip is over.

Good casting requires skill, and skill in almost anything requires both practice and study. It therefore follows, if my logic is in order, that good casting requires practice and study.

What is not logical, however, is that many fishermen think that they can learn to cast well without either. They just want to go fishing . . . and they do!

Nothing wrong with going fishing, but the sad part is that it's difficult to enjoy a fishing trip if you're backlashing every other cast, or find your fly hung ten feet up in a tree when the cast does go well, or can't cast the reasonable distance necessary to reach a feeding fish.

Golfers spend hours on the putting green and more hours hitting balls on the practice fairway! Beginning riflemen and scattergunners fire many shells at clay targets and punch countless holes in paper targets! Bowhunters follow a religious course of getting their archery muscles in condition, spending hours of roving through the woods shooting at targets from various positions! All of them read all they can find about their particular activity.

But most beginning fishermen just go fishing!

If a novice had two weeks to fish, he'd put more on the stringer if he spent the first week in the back yard practice casting, and his evenings cuddled up with a good illustrated book on how to cast and how to fish.

To cast easily and successfully an angler should have well balanced, efficient equipment; he should have that equipment properly assembled and in good condition; and, finally, he should have acquired the skill necessary to use it. All of this, of course, is entirely apart from any knowledge of how to catch a fish.

The three methods of casting, in the order in which they become important in this country, are fly fishing, bait casting, and spinning. Let's examine them in that order.

Fly Casting—the rod and the line are the two important items of equipment. The reel serves to hold the line. In actual fishing large fish are played from the fly reel, of course, but here we are speaking only of the casting.

The proper size fly rod, usually from seven and one-half to nine and one-half feet in length, is selected by the angler for his specific brand of fishing. After that the proper size line is selected for that rod. The right combination will bring out the action of the rod without overburdening it, for in fly casting it is actually the line itself which you are casting. If you have a lure on the end it's just going along for the ride.

It would be most helpful for beginning fly fishermen to watch anglers like Tom McNally, Bob Zwirz or Joe Brooks at "work." Watching the easy rhythm and unhurried grace of these superb casters has a soothing, beneficial effect on the novice, many of whom have the idea that fly fishing is a frantic thing.

There are four basic steps in the fly cast: the pickup, the backcast, the pause, and the forward cast. All are equally important, since poor execution of any of them makes satisfactory casting impossible.

Begin the pickup with the rod almost parallel to the water, with both arms fairly well extended before you. The left hand holds the fly line at a point near the rod handle, and will continue to hold it firmly (we're not concerned with "shooting" line here) until the forward cast is made.

Keeping wrist firm, raise the forearm slowly until the fly line is free of the water, with only the fly itself skittering along the surface toward you. Then apply power smartly to begin the backcast, ending with a flip that sends the line soaring high over your shoulder.

Cease the power of your backcast as the rod passes the vertical point. The rod itself can ride on back to the one or two o'clock position, but no farther.

Pause . . . to give the line time to roll out in the air behind you, with elbow at about shoulder height and wrist still firm. Practice, developing a sense of feel and timing, will ultimately

Free-spool, star—drag bait casting reels work well on the big ones. John Wilhelm takes a good snork in Florida.

At ten, his daughter displays excellent casting, spinning or spin-casting form—reel handle up; forearm and wrist in formal cast; no "pause"; vertical cast; and eyes on target.

tell you when to begin the forward cast.

For the forward cast drop the elbow somewhat and push the rod forward, aiming at a point ten or fifteen feet higher than the actual spot where you want the fly to fall. The forward cast is largely a forearm motion, but ends with a slight wrist action.

Stop the rod at about a 45 degree angle until the fly touches the water, then lower it slightly to the best position for working the lure and to be in position for the next cast.

Pitfalls to avoid in fly casting: 1. trying to pick up a fly line from the water suddenly; 2. taking the rod back too far on the backcast, either from carrying the forearm too far back or from breaking the wrist; 3. failure to pause the proper length of time between backcast and forward cast; 4. chopping downward toward the water on the forward cast rather than pushing the rod out toward your target.

There are many variations of the fly cast to cope with unusual fishing conditions, but the angler who learns the fundamental cast thoroughly will have no trouble mastering them.

Bait Casting—Bait casting as we now know it was developed in this country, with the first multiplying casting reels being made by George Snyder, of Paris, Kentucky, about 1805.

In contrast to fly casting, the bait casting reel is as important as is the bait casting rod, if not more so. Here you are actually casting a lure which pulls the line out after it. The problem is to develop skill enough to let the line feed smoothly off a revolving spool. If the spool revolves faster than the lure is pulling the line out you have a backlash.

Most casting rods should range from five to six and one-half feet in length, with the shorter rods handling heavier lures best. A great variety of casting reels is available now, featuring such fine innovations as lightweight spools to minimize the flywheel effect which tends to cause backlashes, and freespool features which make longer casts with lighter lures practical.

Most casting reels have devices intended to prevent or minimize backlashes—overruns. Used properly they are effective, but all decrease the efficiency of the reel. The beginning angler will find the use of these devices most helpful until his thumb becomes properly educated.

In casting the handles of the reel should be up at the beginning of the cast, for three reasons. First is that the reel itself is more efficient in that position. Second, and more important, this position permits the wrist to work freely. Third, and of utmost importance, in this position the thumb can provide the delicate braking of the spool that is vital.

Begin the basic cast with the rod pointing toward your target at about a 45 degree elevation, with your thumb firmly on the spool. With a combination forearm and wrist movement bring the rod directly up and back for the backcast. Stop the backcast at a point somewhere between one and three o'clock, and immediately begin the forward cast.

A pause between the two movements in bait casting is as fatal as it is necessary to fly casting.

Forearm and wrist movement, again, are used on the forward cast. Stop applying power at about the ten o'clock position and release your thumb from the spool at the same time. The lure will shoot out toward the target, and as it begins to slow down the thumb must be lightly applied to the spool to prevent overrun.

Excellent casting lines of many materials are now available. Use in strengths of eight to twenty pounds, depending upon the lure weight you plan to cast, the kind of fish you plan to fish for, and the type of waters you'll be angling in.

Of extreme importance to smooth bait casting is this: keep your casting reel filled with line. You don't need the length of that much line for fishing, but a full spool has to revolve far fewer times to lay out an equivalent cast than does one only half full.

Pitfalls to avoid in bait casting: 1. casting with your thumb up when making the basic, vertical cast; 2. bringing the rod too far back on the backcast, although this is not as critical as it is in fly casting; 3. pausing between backcast and forward cast; 4. failure to thumb the reel properly.

Spinning—Although spinning was a popular method of fishing in Europe for a hundred years prior to 1945, it was not until World War II ended in that year that this form of angling began to become popular in this country. In less than a decade following that, however, it had swept through the states like wildfire.

Spinning is similar to bait casting in that a lure is cast, pulling line off a reel. The rod is usually from six to seven and one-half feet in length, midway between the bait rod and the fly rod. The actual casting movements in spinning are very similar to those of bait casting.

It is in the spinning reel that the great difference lies. The spool on which the line is wound does not revolve. The line merely feeds off the end of the spool as would sewing thread pulled from its spool.

With no revolving spool there can be no flywheel action, therefore no backlash. As the lure slows down during the cast the line simply feeds off the spool more slowly, then stops as the lure touches the water.

As with bait casting, the procedure for spinning consists only of a backcast and a forward cast. Assume the same wrist and arm position that you would for bait casting. Here, however, the reel is mounted beneath the rod, and you are holding the line with your forefinger rather than thumbing the spool.

Make your backcast and forcast as you would with bait casting, releasing the line from your finger at the appropriate time to shoot the lure toward the target. With the longer rod you'll find that less backcast is needed, and with the spinning reel you'll find that a later release point is needed.

To stop your lure in the air you can make one turn on the reel handle, which engages the bait and stops the lure flight abruptly. More delicate "thumbing" can be done by using your forefinger which released the line to feather it.

Spin-casting is an American adaptation of spinning that features a fixed spool inside a closed cover. It's usually placed on a rod as is a casting reel, and has a push button for thumbing. The casting procedure is virtually the same as for spinning.

An expert caster is not necessarily a good fisherman. More things enter into it than the mere ability to place a lure properly. But when you see your neighbor sitting in his yard casting a hookless plug at an old bicycle tire, think before you shake your head. Odds are he's also got a freezer full of fish.

Bait casting tackle is ideal in situations such as this. Here the largemouths literally have to be dragged out the lily pads, and bait casting gear has the guts to do it.

CHAPTER VI

TACKLE TALK

By Milt Rosko

I shudder whenever I hear someone refer to a fishing rod as a "pole." More often than not the person calling a rod a pole has little background in fishing, for those who follow this finest of participant sports quickly learn that there is a world of difference between the two.

A pole is the thing Huck Finn used in his era. A sapling was cut, a piece of twine affixed to it and a hook and fat old nightcrawler balanced off the terminal end. A fishing rod, on the other hand, is a tool designed expressly to making fishing more enjoyable. Some rods are designed to cast a tiny fly whose weight is infinitesimal, while others comfortably handle a lure weighing five-eighths of an ounce or more. Other rods aren't designed for casting at all, but instead serve a purpose as an angler jigs through the ice, or perhaps trolls in a deep lake or river.

So you see, there's a little more to fishing tackle than just going out and buying a "pole," as some people might lead you to believe.

Basically, in fresh water, we have three types of fishing outfits: spinning, bait casting and fly casting. Each of these is designed for a specific purpose. While each overlaps somewhat, the angler who is a master of each, and who carries these varied outfits with him whenever he goes fishing, will derive more enjoyment from his days astream. I like to compare my selection of fishing equipment to the bag full of clubs a golfer carries. Surely a golfer would be lost if he only had one wood, or perhaps a single iron in his bag. Such is the parallel.

Enough for the background. Now let's get down to specifics on just how to select these basic outfits, so that you'll be able to handle every situation which may arise on the fresh water scene, whether it be lazy old largemouths in a weed choked lake, or vitality sparked rainbows on a fast running mountain stream.

Spinning—I'm a firm believer that you can enjoy something more if at first you find it not too difficult. So, for a starter I'd suggest giving the nod to spinning, as such an outfit is very easy to master, and it is a deadly way of taking many of our fine gamefish.

A spinning outfit is primarily a casting combination, so designed to enable you to present lures ranging from one-sixteenth of an ounce and up with a minimum of effort. You'll find a wide selection of spinning outfits available at your local tackle shop, but for all practical purposes they fall into two categories: medium weight spinning, which I believe is the best choice for the beginner, and ultra light spinning, which is fine once you've mastered the former.

For an all-around fresh water spinning rod I'm partial to one measuring six feet, six inches, to seven feet overall. It should be classified by its manufacturer as having a light to medium action, built to handle lures ranging from one-quarter to one-half ounce. A rod such as this can be purchased in a price range from two to two hundred dollars, and I'm not exaggerating when I say this!

The important thing to remember when putting together an outfit is to purchase the best you can afford. Don't buy an expensive rod, and a cheap reel. Purchase all of the items within the range that doesn't hurt your pocketbook, but bear in mind that spending a little more at the start may be economical in the long run.

Let's run down a few of the items you should watch for when selecting a spinning rod. There are shafts of many materials on the market, but for my money I'll stick to hollow fiberglass, as it is lightweight, durable, and economical. Cheaper rods are often one piece, but keep in mind they're difficult to store, so it might be worth the extra couple of dollars to get one with a ferrule. Look for a rod which has five or six graduated spinning guides, so that the strain of casting, or fighting fish, is evenly distributed throughout the rod. While some manufacturers will hate me for saying so, stay away from agate guides! Regardless of what is said, they do break. And believe me, nothing spoils a day like a broken guide several miles from the car. I stick with quality stainless steel, and periodically check them for wear.

The handle of the rod should be of quality species cork, or a good quality cork composition. Look the handle over carefully. If the cork seems to have rather big holes in it you'll find it will quickly rot and fall apart. Make certain the

Here the angler works a stretch of stream choked with weeds and trees along the banks. This rules out a fly rod, but a spinning rig works wonders with trout that are hanging in the shade of the foliage.

A tiny nymph fished with a fly rod by outdoor scribe Henry Schaefer accounted for this fine golden trout in West Virginia.

butt has some sort of a metal, plastic or rubber cap on it, as just plain cork will chip off or wear without the protective cap.

There are those who still prefer a spinning stick without a fixed reel seat, but I am not one of them. I like a good quality, lightweight anodized screw locking reel seat. The reason is very simple. It holds the reel firmly and securely, which makes for comfortable fishing.

Make certain you don't purchase a rod because of all the frills. Windings, decals, protective flannel bags, aluminum or fiber tubes, and the like are all gimmicks to get you to buy, but they don't make it a better rod. Rather you get a plain rod that's a quality one, than get a mediocre stick that's been made eye-appealing by a marketing tycoon.

When we get into spinning reels we get into another problem of marketing. Little does the newcomer realize that fishing tackle is big business, and as such everyone is putting out a gimmick to sell his particular product. I, for one, don't believe in gimmicks. There are spinning reels with closed faces, open faces; bails that open by themselves and others which are manual; some have drags in the front, while others have them in the back, and there are even star drags; some are fast retrieve, while others are slow. I could go on and on, but I'd rather say these gadgets and features don't necessarily catch fish. In fact they'll often cause you a lot of grief.

I prefer a very basic reel. Many spinning reels have a full bail, which is fine when it's working. But being a moving part, attached in a way which makes it vulnerable to being accidentally hit, makes it a nuisance. On the reels I use I usually have the bail removed and a manual pick-up put on. In effect, all this means is that I have to pick up the line with my finger when I start to retrieve. Once you get used to it it's a charm.

I like a reel which has a push-button spool release, as this makes for quick changing of spools, and enables me to carry several extra spools of line with me at all times. The drag is built right into the spool, and once you set it you needn't change it, even after removing the spool from the reel. It also has a conveniently located anti-reverse lever, and a one-shot lubrication system which makes for easy maintenance. Speaking of maintenance, make certain you select a well-known name, by a reputable manufacturer or importer, so that parts and service are available. There are several reels on the market for which replacement parts just aren't available.

The spinning reel I find to my liking is available with a large and small capacity spool. While fishing lakes and big water I use the large spools, which I load with 250 yards of eight-pound test monofilament, while on streams and ponds I find the small capacity spool holding 175 yards of four-pound line or 125 yards of six-pound test is ideal.

Bait Casting—For a while spinning stole much of the glory from bait casting, but now more than ever the dyed-in-the-wool angler is realizing there is an important place for this fine outfit on certain angling waters.

For the most part, bait casting is a little on the heavier side than spinning. It is more useful on big, open water than in confining places. It just has no peer on big rivers where musky and steelhead abound, or on lakes where big bass and pickerel spend most of their time in the protected reaches of lily pads. Very simply put, a bait casting outfit has guts!

I have a tendency to stick with a bait casting rod that measures in the vicinity of six feet overall. I find the rods that measure over this length are often unwieldly and difficult to handle fish with, particularly when fishing alone. Much the same as with spinning, I find a two-piece rod to my liking, and it should have four or five stainless steel guides to distribute the strain throughout the entire rod.

I like a rod which has what is known as a fast taper tip. In effect this means the tip is light and flexible, yet the butt section has plenty of backbone. This enables you to handle a wide range of lure weights with ease. As a rule I find myself handling lures from one-quarter ounce to five-eights of an ounce with little difficulty. If the tip is too stiff, you'll often encounter trouble handling the one-quarter ounce lures.

There isn't too wide a range in the handles found on bait casting rods. For the most part they have an offset reel seat, which puts the reel in such a position that the line flows smoothly from reel right down into the first guide. The handle itself is more often than not covered with specie cork, or composition cork. Here again, make certain it is quality.

Of all the many types of fishing equipment made for fresh water anglers I believe that the finest piece is the bait casting reel. I wouldn't be far wrong in saying that more work has gone into the perfection of the bait casting reel than any other item of fishing tackle, much to the delight of the angling public.

I used an imported "knuckle-buster" that's a honey. It has a smooth as silk level-wind mechanism, a free spool which automatically engages when the retrieve is started and a centrifugal brake which lets me reach out with nice long casts. It also has an adjustable mechanical brake, which proves advantageous when swinging from one bait size to another, let's say from a quarter-ounce lure to a live bait rig that may weigh close to two ounces.

The reel has a quick take-apart feature, which enables me to carry two spools of line for quick changing. For bait casting I usually use braided nylon, or more recently, braided dacron lines. I load one spool with 125 yards of ten-pound test line and the other with 100 yards of fifteen-pound test which usually covers every angling situation I might run into. Of course, I would like to qualify this by saying that in really bad spots, such as stump filled lakes, or where weed growth is extremely heavy, I do on occasion use as heavy as 20- or 25-pound test line. More as an economy feature so I don't have to break off lures, and/or fish.

It takes a bit of practice to master a multiplying reel. For those who don't have the time, or patience, there are spincasting reels which work out very nicely with a conventional bait casting rod. Spin-casting with a closed-faced reel is much the same as bait casting, only a lot easier. Here the line leaves the fixed spool of a reel, which doesn't require the sensitive thumbing of a multiplying reel.

Fly Casting—In fly casting we have the ultimate in fresh water fishing. All fresh water fish will take a fly, and once you've caught one on a little tuft of feathers you'll be hooked for life. It doesn't much matter whether it be a small trout on a local brook or a majestic salmon on a wild virgin river.

There are a variety of fly casting outfits available, but we'll try to cover an all-around outfit best suited to average fishing conditions. This will rule out the outfits for big salmon rivers, and the bugging outfits, or the tiny miniature outfits for very small water.

Perhaps more than with any rod, reel and line combination, balance is uppermost when you select a fly rod. In effect, you are throwing the line with the aid of the rod. To do this the rod and line must be balanced to each other. With fly lines, their weight is the important factor. Thus, with too heavy a line the rod won't handle it, and neither will it handle a line that is too light. A rod will only handle certain weight lines properly, and never let anyone lead you to believe otherwise.

Here is where it is difficult to put down on paper just what combination is the ideal outfit. You see, manufacturers don't match their outfits correctly. I'd venture a guess that fully half of the fly rods manufactured today are marked for lines which really and truly don't balance with them. The only way you can match up an outfit is to purchase the rod, line and reel from a tackle shop where you know they are experts with fly-fishing equipment. Don't make the mistake of going into a discount house and asking the clerk behind the counter for a fly rod outfit! You'll go home with a rig that will wrap the line around your neck, and that's about all.

A rod that I've found to be a good all around choice for a variety of conditions is an eight-foot dry fly action rod. It is two piece and made of fiberglass, weighing in at four ounces. On this particular rod HDH double taper or HCF torpedo taper handles delightfully. Let me caution you that in selecting any fly rod, give it a try first, or use the outfit of a friend which works well, and buy the exact duplicate.

Among the important things to look for in a fly rod are a not too sloppy tip action, a fast taper tip and quality, light-weight hardware. Guides should be well distributed, with most rods measuring eight feet having approximately seven snake guides and one large stripper guide.

Selection of a reel to balance with your rod is not too much of a problem. There are several excellent reels made in America as well as a fine selection of imported models. In a few specialized types of fishing you will fight the fish from the fly wheel, but these situations are not the everyday oc-curance. We find a three and a half inch single action reel just right for the rod discussed. It's a quality reel precision machined with a one-piece frame, and it has a good line guard and a smooth working drag for those occasions when I need it. The spool is ventilated for quick drying of any accumulated water and it has an instant spool removal fea-ture that makes it a snap to clean and oil.

While we've covered just the basic fundamentals of select-ing a fresh water spin, bait or fly casting outfit, I'd like to strongly recommend that you put your confidence in a reputable tackle dealer and have him assist you in selecting the best outfits for your particular needs. Remember that many things enter into the picture, starting from your physical size, the type of water you plan to fish most frequently, and the size and varieties of fish which are available in these waters.

Many years ago Huck Finn simply cut himself a "pole" and went fishing! Today, there's a lot more to it than that.

By realizing this and selecting your fishing tackle accordingly, you'll get a great deal more out of each and every day you spend on the water.

Streamers and bucktails, sometimes called simply large wet flies, are killers on all game fish of fresh and salt water. The reason for the variety of patterns shown here is an attempt to imitate the various and sometimes very specific minnows and bait fish upon which the game fish feed. Then there is the business of dressing for surface fishing, when the fly is bulky and will ride high. At other times it is best to dress the flies sparsely so they will sink deeper and work more delicately, especially when fished in gin-clear water. A heavier leader is used with these flies than with the smaller and more delicate wet and dry flies. When the fish hits one of these flies it is generally on the retrieve when the angler is working the fly back toward him. Under this stress a big fish smacks it hard. A light leader would be apt to break. Least size leader strength is four pounds test.

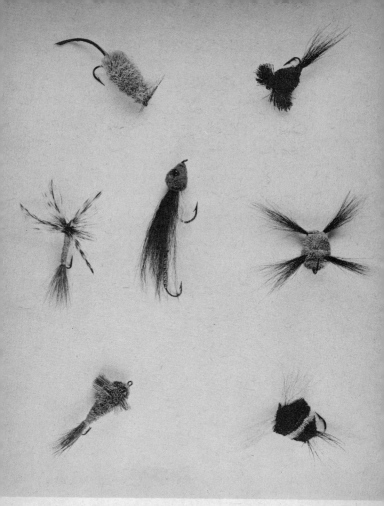

These are bass bugs and surface popping flies used primarily in large and smallmouth bass fishing from Florida to Ontario. They are generally fished in the shallows or in close to the weed patches and snags. A stout fly rod of at least nine feet in length with a heavy or fast action tip is recommended. A line of at least GAF taper is needed. A short level leader testing five pounds is recommended and need not be longer than five feet.

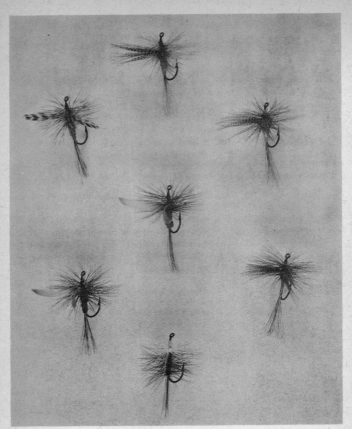

Dry flies of these varied types of dressing are used primarily for stream and lake fishing for trout. Best times are morning and evening when the fish are seen to be rising after insects that are either hatching from the surface or landing from their flights in the sky. A light long tapered leader is needed to cast them delicately to the fish. In stream fishing in clear water, extremely light and long leaders are required with a rod and line to match. Spinning lures are used for a variety of fresh and salt water fish. Trout, bass, pickerel, pike, musky and panfish will take them trolled or cast. Reason for the variety is to imitate the fish that the gamesters are taking at the moment. Often it is just a matter of the lure's action and speed of the angler's retrieve that will provoke a strike. This assortment is typical of the variety needed to complete the average angler's collection.

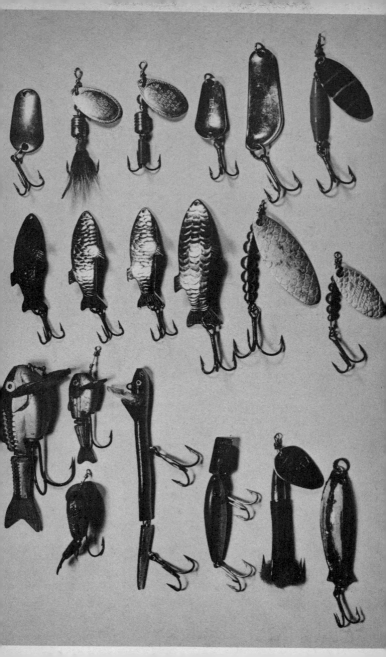

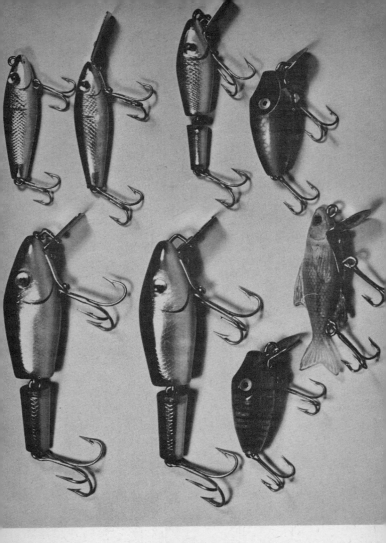

Jointed plugs of the popping, diving, zig-zagging types are especially attractive to bass. They can be fished either with spinning gear or bait casting tackle, trolled or cast, depending on the conditions and also the whim of the angler. Here, color, action, speed of retrieve or troll will often make the difference in the action from the fish. Start with a generous and varied collection.

This fly fisherman had his hands full when he hooked this nine-pound brown trout on the LeTort Spring Run in Pennsylvania, but he took his time, and let the fish have his head until he was well tired. By carefully playing the fish on the small size 12 fly and 3x tippet he brought it within reach with his two-ounce fly rod, and managed to get his hand in its gill.

CHAPTER VII

FRESH-WATER FISHING—WHEN AND WHERE

By Jack Seville

When to go fishing? One of the best anglers I know always says the best time is "right now." Had he in the same breath been asked where, he'd undoubtedly have named the nearest body of water. Actually there is more than jest in these remarks. Safely assuming that the reader of this book is interested in the fun of fishing and the enjoyment of being out of doors, why not go whenever you can grab the time and why overlook the waters close to home?

At one time I had the good fortune to live right on a good bass lake. It annoyed me some that I had to leave it every day to work in the nearby city. I could only fish when time permitted. Once in a while I was able to drag myself out of bed a little early for a few early-morning casts. More often I contented myself with some early evening fishing. Actually, of necessity, I fished the best times of day. And for the beginner, that is something worth remembering . . . generally, fish are least active in mid-day. As a matter of fact, for those who like it, nighttime fishing will often bring best results. It is not particularly appealing to me—mainly because I enjoy seeing the action.

Fish are where you find them and there is a great deal of satisfaction in finding them on your own. Often, by following a familiar stream back away from the road you can find good fishing within earshot of the cars dashing off to some distant "hot-spot." Quiet little ponds and deserted quarry pits a stone's throw from a busy highway might give up a trophy bass. Until a very few years ago, because attention was focused on bigger water and bigger fish close at hand, there were almost-virgin ponds on Long Island and the Eastern Shore of the Chesapeake Bay. Since then, articles by enlightened fishermen have been published on the subject and still those ponds can stand more fishing.

74

Most of the country has been well mapped by the U.S. Corps of Engineers. Through the U.S. Coast and Geodetic Survey you can get those detailed findings in the form of topographic quadrangles. They will show you some water in your area you may not have known existed—possibly even floatable streams, and if you haven't float-fished, you have missed a delightful, leisurely way of doing it.

Don't overlook any water. For years I had heard that abandoned pits left by strip-mining and borrow pits, given time and the wonderful ways of Nature, can produce amazing strings of fish. When the Everglades National Park was established I was invited to Cape Sable to have a look and fish for snook and tarpon. To get there means a drive of 39 miles through a prairie of sawgrass and water. To fill and construct the road, the builders left a number of "borrow" pits. After a couple of days of smash-bang fishing for tarpon and snook in the mangrove islands, I suggested to my host we try those pits for bass.

"Hell, man," he said, "there's not a thing but water in those pits and we've got oceans of tarpon yonder." He wrote me a couple of months later that he couldn't get that whacky idea out of his head and just had to try pit fishing to prove my notion wrong. He was happy to confess that he caught bass.

If your business requires traveling, get in the habit of packing a compact fishing kit. A suitcase rod and a few bass lures, no matter where you tote them in this country, will rarely be far from fishable water. Who knows, a little fishing talk when you arrive at your destination could be the entree you need to complete your business successfully!

And that fishing talk is an important route to good fishing, too. Check in with the local tackle dealers; they practically have to know where the fish are. They can also tell you the lures and methods used successfully in that area. When you can plan in advance, the local Chamber of Commerce might be of help too. And don't forget the conservation department of the state to be visited. You will need their information on license, seasons and limits. They can also tell you where to go for fish. Contact the fish warden. He knows the area intimately and is there to help, not hinder, anglers.

If the lure of faraway places still burns within, don't fret. Most of the best commercial fishing camps advertise in the outdoor magazines. Generally speaking, you are safe in following these leads. A resort operator has to have something worth offering or he won't last long enough to be able to afford the advertising.

Happily, too, there are still places you can go without having to pay an arm and a leg. The network of National Wildlife Refuges, Parks and Forests total some 200 million acres and includes some of the country's best fishing. Current information on these public lands is best obtained by writing to the resident manager of the individual areas. Often there are camping or cabin facilities maintained for public use or commercial lodging nearby. Your own state probably also has commonwealth-owned lands set aside for fishermen. Surprisingly, many of these public facilities are under fished.

SOURCE OF FISHING INFORMATION

The following list has been compiled for a ready source of up-to-date information on States and National Forests, their laws, and in many cases free booklets on where to go for each species of game fish. This information may be had for the asking. The same is true for the Canadian listings.

Alabama—Department of Conservation, Administrative Building, Montgomery, Ala.

Alaska—Department of Fish and Game, 229 Alaska Office Building, Juneau, Alaska.

Arizona—State Game and Fish Commission, Arizona State Building, Phoenix, Ariz.

Arkansas—State Game and Fish Commission, Game and Fish Building, State Capitol Grounds, Little Rock, Ark.

California—Department of Fish and Game, 722 Capitol Avenue, Sacramento, Calif.

Colorado—State Game and Fish Department, 1530 Sherman St., Denver 2, Colo.

Connecticut—State Board of Fisheries and Game, State Office Building, Hartford 14, Conn.

Delaware—Board of Game and Fish Commissioners, Dover, Del.

District of Columbia—Metropolitan Police, Washington, has jurisdiction.

Florida—Game and Fresh Water Fish Commission, 646 W. Tennessee, Tallahassee, Fla.

Georgia—State Game and Fish Commission, 401 State Capitol, Atlanta 3, Ga.

Hawaii—Board of Commissioners of Agriculture and Forestry, Division of Fish and Game, Box 5425, Pawaa Substation, Honolulu 1, Hawaii.

Idaho—Department of Fish and Game, 518 Front St., Boise, Ida.

Illinois—Department of Conservation, State Office Building, Springfield, Ill.

Indiana—Department of Conservation Division of Fish and Game, 311 W. Washington St., Indianapolis 9, Ind.

Iowa—State Conservation Commission, E. 7th & Court Ave., Des Moines 9, Ia.

Kansas—Forestry, Fish and Game Commission, Box 591, Pratt, Kans.

Kentucky—Department of Fish and Wildlife Resources, State Office Building, Annex, Frankfort, Ky.

Louisiana—Wild Life and Fisheries Commission, 126 Civil Courts Building, New Orleans 16, La.

Maine—Department of Inland Fisheries and Game, State House, Augusta, Me.

Maryland—Maryland Game and Inland Fish Commission, State Office Building, Annapolis, Md.

Massachusetts—Department of Natural Resources, Division of Fisheries and Game, 73 Tremont St., Boston 8, Mass.

Michigan—Department of Conservation, Lansing 26, Mich.

Minnesota—Department of Conservation, State Office Building, St. Paul 1, Minn.

Mississippi—State Game and Fish Commission, Woolfolk State Office Building, Jackson, Miss.

Missouri—State Conservation Commission, Farm Bureau Building, Jefferson City, Mo.

Montana—State Fish and Game Commission, Helena, Mont.

Nebraska—Game, Forestation and Parks Commission, State Capitol Building, Lincoln 9, Neb.

Nevada—State Fish and Game Commission, Box 678, Reno, Nev.

New Hampshire—State Fish and Game Department, 34 Bridge St., Concord, N. H.

New Jersey—Department of Conservation and Economic Development, Division of Fish and Game, 230 West State St., Trenton, N. J.

New Mexico—State Department of Game and Fish, Santa Fe, N. M.

New York—State Conservation Department, Albany, N. Y.

North Carolina—Wildlife Resources Commission, Box 2919, Raleigh, N. C.

North Dakota—State Game and Fish Department, Bismarck, N. D.

Ohio—Department of Natural Resources, Wildlife Division, Ohio Department Building, Columbus 15, Ohio.

Oklahoma—Department of Wildlife Conservation, Room 118, State Capitol Building, Oklahoma City 5, Okla.

Oregon—State Fish Commission, 307 State Office Building, Portland 1, Ore.

Pennsylvania—State Fish Commission, Harrisburg, Pa.

Puerto Rico—Department of Agriculture and Commerce, San Juan, P. R.

Rhode Island—Department of Agriculture and Conservation, Veterans Memorial Building, 83 Park St., Providence 2, R. I.

South Carolina—State Wildlife Resources Department, 1015 Main St., Box 360, Columbia, S. C.

South Dakota—State Department of Game, Fish and Parks, State Office Building, Pierre, S. D.

Tennessee—State Game and Fish Commission, Cordell Hull Building, Nashville, Tenn.

Texas—State Game and Fish Commission, Austin, Tex.

Utah—State Department of Fish and Game, 1596 W. N. Temple, Salt Lake City, Utah.

Vermont—State Fish and Game Commission, Montpelier, Vt.

Virginia—Commission of Game and Inland Fisheries, 7 N. 2nd St., Box 1642, Richmond 13, Va.

Washington—Department of Game, 600 N. Capitol Way, Olympia, Wash.

West Virginia—State Conservation Commission, State Office Building, No. 3, Charleston, W. Va.

Wisconsin—State Conservation Department, State Office Building, Madison 1, Wis.

Wyoming—State Game and Fish Commission, Box 378, Cheyenne, Wyo.

CANADA:

Alberta—Department of Lands and Forests, Edmonton, Alta.

British Columbia—Fish and Game Branch, Department of Recreation and Conservation, 567 Burrard St., Vancouver 1, B. C.

Manitoba—Department of Mines and Natural Resources, Winnipeg, Man.

New Brunswick — Department of Travel Information, Fredericton, New Brunswick.

Newfoundland—Department of Mines and Resources, St. John's, Newfoundland.

Northwest Territories—Northern Administration Branch, Department of Northern Affairs and National Resources, Ottawa, Ontario.

Nova Scotia—Department of Lands and Forests, Halifax, N. S.

Ontario—Department of Lands and Forests, Parliament Buildings, Toronto, Ontario.

Prince Edward Island—Department of Industry and Natural Resources, Charlottetown, P.E.I.

Quebec—Department of Game and Fisheries, Quebec, Que.

Saskatchewan—Department of Natural Resources, Government Administration Building, Regina, Sask.

Yukon Territory—Game Department, Yukon Territorial Government, Box 2029, Whitehorse, Y. T., Canada.

MAPS THAT AID THE ANGLER:

The federal government offers us the finest maps available. Each state is divided into small areas and a separate map is available for each. Each stream, river and lake is shown in detail as are dirt roads and little known access areas.

For maps east of the Mississippi River, contact the Geological Survey, Washington 25, D.C. West of the Mississippi, contact Geological Survey, Federal Center, Denver, Colorado.

Index maps of each state are available, free, which show all the quadrangles available for each area. From these master maps you may choose the individual area you wish to fish—then order it, by number, from Geological Survey for 30 cents per map.

National Forests are a particularly good bet for fishermen who are looking for beautiful scenery as well as excellent angling. Here is a list of our top spots in the United States:

A good 35 MM camera such as this Miranda should be a part of the angler's gear. A good photograph of your catch is nice to have in the album and will also help you to prove your fish stories.

ALABAMA

WILLIAM B. BANKHEAD NATIONAL FOREST, 178,-895 acres, Montgomery, Ala. Bass and bream. *GOOD*

CONCUH NATIONAL FOREST, 83,790 acres, Montgomery, Ala. Bass and bream. *FAIR*

TALLADEGA NATIONAL FOREST, 357,847 acres, Montgomery, Ala. Bass and bream. *GOOD*

TUSKEGEE NATIONAL FOREST, 10,777 acres, Montgomery, Ala. Bream. *FAIR*

ALASKA

CHUGACH NATIONAL FOREST, 4,726,145 acres, Anchorage, Alaska. Trout. *FAIR*

TONGASS NATIONAL FOREST, North Division 16,-016,140 acres, Juneau, Alaska. Trout. *GOOD*

TONGASS NATIONAL FOREST, South Division, 16,-016,140 acres, Ketchikan, Alaska. Trout.

ARIZONA

APACHE NATIONAL FOREST, partly in New Mexico, acres, Springerville, Ariz. Trout fishing. *GOOD*

COCONINO NATIONAL FOREST, 1,801,091 acres, Flagstaff, Ariz. Lake and stream fishing. *FAIR*

CORONADO NATIONAL FOREST, partly in New Mexico, 1,196,534 acres, Tucson, Ariz. Trout and bass fishing. *GOOD*

KAIBAB NATIONAL FOREST, 1,715,190 acres, Williams, Ariz. *FAIR*

PRESCOTT NATIONAL FOREST, 1,248,210 acres, Prescott, Ariz. Trout fishing. *FAIR*

SITGREAVES NATIONAL FOREST, 744,820 acres, Holbrook, Ariz. *POOR*

TONTO NATIONAL FOREST, 2,902,072 acres, Phoenix, Ariz. Artificial lakes covering 30,000 acres. Bass and trout fishing. *GOOD*

ARKANSAS

OUACHITA NATIONAL FOREST, partly in Oklahoma, 1,542,412 acres, Hot Springs, Ark. Bass. *GOOD*

OZARK NATIONAL FOREST, 1,046,309 acres, Russelville, Ark. Stream and lake fishing. *FAIR*

CALIFORNIA

ANGELES NATIONAL FOREST, 648,754 acres, Pasadena, Calif.   *FAIR*

CLEVELAND NATIONAL FOREST, 391,682 acres, San Diego, Calif.   *FAIR*

ELDORADO NATIONAL FOREST, 640,619 acres, Placerville, Calif. Lake and stream fishing.   *FAIR*

INYO NATIONAL FOREST, 1,774,176 acres, partly in Nevada, Bishop, Calif. Lake and stream fishing.

KLAMATH NATIONAL FOREST, partly in Oregon, 1,697,600 acres. Yreka, Calif. Klamath River and tributaries with salmon and steelhead fishing. Also trout.

LASSEN NATIONAL FOREST, 1,047,372 acres, Susanville, Calif. Lake and stream fishing for rainbows, Loch Leven, and steelhead trout.

LOS PADRES NATIONAL FOREST, 1,740,245 acres, Santa Barbara, Calif. Trout.   *FAIR*

MENDOCINO NATIONAL FOREST, 867,425 acres, Willows, Calif. Stream fishing.   *GOOD*

MODOC NATIONAL FOREST, 1,688,789 acres, Alturas, Calif.   *GOOD*

PLUMAS NATIONAL FOREST, 1,147,611 acres, Quincy, Calif. The famous Feather River country. Trout fishing, lakes, streams.   *EXCELLENT*

SAN BERNARDINO NATIONAL FOREST, 613,912 acres, San Bernardino, Calif. Lake and stream fishing.

SEQUOIA NATIONAL FOREST, 1,118,551 acres, Porterville, Calif. Golden trout and usual trout species.
                                                        GOOD

SHASTA-TRINITY NATIONAL FOREST, 2,036,836 acres, Redding, Calif. Lake and streams, golden trout and usual trout species.

SIERRA NATIONAL FOREST, 1,295,832 acres, Fresno, Calif. Lake and stream.   *GOOD*

SIX RIVERS NATIONAL FOREST, 935,268 acres, Eureka, Calif. Trout fishing in spring and summer; steelhead and salmon fishing in fall and winter.
                                                   EXCELLENT

STANISLAUS NATIONAL FOREST, 896,165 acres, Sonora, Calif.   *EXCELLENT*

TAHOE NATIONAL FOREST, 694,112 acres, Nevada City, Calif. Lake and stream fishing.

COLORADO

ARAPAHO NATIONAL FOREST, 990,371 acres, Golden, Colo. Lake and stream fishing.

GRAND MESA-UNCOMPAHGRE NATIONAL FORESTS, 1,317,865 acres, Delta, Colo. Lake and stream fishing.

GUNNISON NATIONAL FOREST, 1,660,147 acres, Gunnison, Colo. Trout.   *GOOD*

PIKE NATIONAL FOREST, 1,084,947 acres, Colorado Springs, Colo. Lake and stream fishing.

RIO GRANDE NATIONAL FOREST, 1,800,322 acres, Monte Vista, Colo. Trout, high lakes and stream.

ROOSEVELT NATIONAL FOREST, 784,050 acres, Fort Collins, Colo. Trout fishing, lakes, streams.

ROUTT NATIONAL FOREST, 1,145,111 acres, Steamboat Spring, Colo. Trout, streams, high lakes.

SAN ISABEL NATIONAL FOREST, 1,104,042 acres, Pueblo, Colo. Lake and stream trout fishing.   *GOOD*

SAN JUAN NATIONAL FOREST, 1,850,053 acres, Durango, Colo. Alpine lakes. Trout fishing.

WHITE RIVER NATIONAL FOREST, 1,961,798 acres, Glenwood Springs, Colo. Trout.   *GOOD*

FLORIDA

APALACHICOLA NATIONAL FOREST, 556,480 acres, Tallahassee, Fla. Bass, bream and perch.

OCALA NATIONAL FOREST, 361,029 acres, Tallahassee, Fla. Bass and bream.   *EXCELLENT*

OSCEOLA NATIONAL FOREST, 157,233 acres, Tallahassee, Fla. Bass, perch and bream.

GEORGIA

CHATTAHOOCHEE NATIONAL FOREST, 680,333 acres, Gainesville, Ga. Trout and bass.

OCONEE NATIONAL FOREST, 96,066 acres, Gainesville, Ga. Bass and bream.

IDAHO

BOISE NATIONAL FOREST, 2,629,465 acres, Boise, Idaho. Trout and salmon.

CARIBOU NATIONAL FOREST, partly in Utah and Wyoming, 976,041 acres, Pocatello, Idaho. Trout.

CHALLIS NATIONAL FOREST, 2,447,696 acres, Challis, Idaho. Trout.

CLEARWATER NATIONAL FOREST, 1,248,455 acres, Orofino, Idaho. Trout.

COEUR D'ALENE NATIONAL FOREST, 723,217 acres, Coeur d'Alene, Idaho. Lake and stream fishing.

KANIKSU NATIONAL FOREST, 1,625,383 acres, partly in Montana and Washington, Sandpoint, Idaho. *GOOD*

NEZPERCE NATIONAL FOREST, 2,195,908 acres, Grangeville, Idaho. Holds famous Selway-Biterrroot Wilderness Area. Trout.

PAYETTE NATIONAL FOREST, 2,307,205 acres, Mc-Call, Idaho. Has 154 fishing lakes, 1,530 miles of fishing streams. Trout.   *EXCELLENT*

SALMON NATIONAL FOREST, 1,768,718 acres, Salmon, Idaho. Trout.

ST. JOE NATIONAL FOREST, 866,269 acres, St. Maries, Idaho. Lake and stream fishing.

SAWTOOTH NATIONAL FOREST, partly in Utah, 1,802,680 acres, Twin Falls, Idaho. Has famous Sun Valley. Trout.

TARGHEE NATIONAL FOREST, partly in Wyoming, 1,666,370 acres, St. Anthony, Idaho. Trout.

ILLINOIS

SHAWNEE NATIONAL FOREST, 211,013 acres, Harrisburg, Ill. River and lake fishing. Bass, panfiish.

INDIANA

HOOSIER NATIONAL FOREST, 117,906 acres, Bedford, Ind. Bass, bluegill, catfish.   *GOOD*

KENTUCKY

CUMBERLAND NATIONAL FOREST, 458,352 acres, Winchester, Ky. Bass, pike, crappie and bluegill. *GOOD*

LOUISIANA

KISATCHIE NATIONAL FOREST, 591,726 acres, Alexandria, La. Bass.   *GOOD*

MICHIGAN

HURON NATIONAL FOREST, 414,819 acres, Cadillac, Mich. Trout.   *EXCELLENT*

MANISTEE NATIONAL FOREST, 445,775 acres, Cadillac, Mich. The Lake Huron National Forest. Bass, pickerel, panfish.   *GOOD*

OTTAWA NATIONAL FOREST, 858,352 acres, Iron-
wood, Mich. Bass and trout.   *GOOD*
HIAWATHA-MARQUETTE NATIONAL FORESTS,
830,179 acres, Escanaba, Mich. Trout, bass, northern
pike, walleyes and perch.   *GOOD*

MINNESOTA
CHIPPEWA NATIONAL FOREST, 639,452 acres, Cass
Lake, Minn. Walleyes, northern pike and panfish. *GOOD*
SUPERIOR NATIONAL FOREST, 1,957,981 acres,
Duluth, Minn. Walleyes, northern pike, bass, trout.
                                          EXCELLENT

MISSISSIPPI—Bass and panfish.
BIENVILLE NATIONAL FOREST, 175,657 acres, Jack-
son, Miss.   *GOOD*
DE SOTO NATIONAL FOREST, 500,335 acres, Jackson,
Miss.   *GOOD*
HOLLY SPRINGS NATIONAL FOREST, 143,352 acres,
Jackson, Miss.   *POOR*
HOMOCHITTO NATIONAL FOREST, 189,069 acres,
Jackson, Miss.   *FAIR*
TOMBIGBEE NATIONAL FOREST, 65,232 acres, Jack-
son, Miss.   *GOOD*

MISSOURI
CLARK NATIONAL FOREST, 902,662 acres, Rolla, Mo.
Smallmouth bass.   *EXCELLENT*
MARK TWAIN NATIONAL FOREST, 451,085 acres,
Rolla, Mo. Bass, walleyes and panfish.   *GOOD*

MONTANA
BEAVERHEAD NATIONAL FOREST, 2,131,136 acres,
Dillon, Mont. Trout, the Big Madison, Big Hole, and
Beaverhead rivers.   *EXCELLENT*
BITTERROOT NATIONAL FOREST, partly in Idaho,
1,574,563 acres, Hamilton, Mont. Trout. *EXCELLENT*
DEERLODGE NATIONAL FOREST, 1,134,639 acres,
Butte, Mont. Trout.   *GOOD*
FLATHEAD NATIONAL FOREST, 2,336,378 acres,
Kalispell, Mont. Trout.   *GOOD*
GALLATIN NATIONAL FOREST, 1,700,139 acres,

Bozeman, Mont. Thousands of miles of fine trout streams. *EXCELLENT*

HELENA NATIONAL FOREST, 966,613 acres, Helena, Mont. Trout. *GOOD*

KOOTENAI NATIONAL FOREST, partly in Idaho, 1,817,975 acres, Libby, Mont. Trout.

LEWIS AND CLARK NATIONAL FOREST, 1,862,011 acres, Great Falls, Mont. Trout. *GOOD*

LOLO NATIONAL FOREST, 2,502,698 acres, partly in Idaho, Missoula, Mont. Trout. *FAIR*

NEBRASKA

NEBRASKA NATIONAL FOREST, 206,082 acres, Lincoln, Nebraska. *FAIR*

NEVADA

HUMBOLDT NATIONAL FOREST, 2,507,869 acres, Elko, Nev. Trout. *FAIR*

TOIYABE NATIONAL FOREST, partly in California, 3,118,966 acres, Reno, Nev. *EXCELLENT*

NEW HAMPSHIRE

WHITE MOUNTAIN NATIONAL FOREST, partly in Maine, 723,394 acres, Laconia, N. H. Brook trout angling.

NEW MEXICO

CARSON NATIONAL FOREST, 1,225,408 acres, Taos, N. M. Trout streams and lakes.

CIBOLA NATIONAL FOREST, 1,696,702 acres, Albuquerque, N. M. *POOR*

GILA NATIONAL FOREST, 2,715,520 acres, Silver City, N. M. Lake fishing in Wall Lake and Bear Canyon Reservoir. Trout. *GOOD*

LINCOLN NATIONAL FOREST, 1,087,855 acres, Alamogordo, N. M. Trout. *FAIR*

SANTA FE NATIONAL FOREST, 1,233,550 acres, Sante Fe, N. M. Trout. *GOOD*

NORTH CAROLINA

CROATAN NATIONAL FOREST, 152,351 acres, Asheville, N. C. Bass and panfish. *FAIR*

NANTAHALA NATIONAL FOREST, 448,278 acres, Asheville, N. C. Trout and bass *GOOD*

PISGAH NATIONAL FOREST, 479,697 acres, Asheville, N. C. Trout and bass   *GOOD*

OHIO
WAYNE NATIONAL FOREST, 106,129 acres, Forest Supervisor, Bedford, Ohio. Bass and panfish.   *GOOD*

OREGON
DESCHUTES NATIONAL FOREST, 1,659,368 acres, Bend, Ore. Rainbow trout.   *GOOD*
FREMONT NATIONAL FOREST, 1,254,595 acres, Lakeview, Ore. Rainbow, brook trout.   *GOOD*
MALHEUR NATIONAL FOREST, 1,410,548 acres, John Day, Ore. Rainbows, steelheads.   *GOOD*
MOUNT HOOD NATIONAL FOREST, 1,115,344 acres, Portland, Ore. Trout.   *GOOD*
OCHOCO NATIONAL FOREST, 845,876 acres, Prineville, Ore. Trout.   *GOOD*
ROGUE RIVER NATIONAL FOREST, partly in California, 839,290 acres, Medford, Ore. Steelhead, rainbows.   *EXCELLENT*
SISKIYOU NATIONAL FOREST, partly in California, 1,046,607 acres, Grants Pass, Ore. Pacific salmon, cutthroats and steelheads.   *EXCELLENT*
SIUSLAW NATIONAL FOREST, 621,044 acres, Corvallis, Ore. Trout.   *FAIR*
UMATILLA NATIONAL FOREST, partly in Washington, 1,075,938 acres, Pendleton, Ore. Steelheads, rainbows.   *EXCELLENT*
UMPQUA NATIONAL FOREST, 978,704 acres, Roseburg, Ore. Steelhead, rainbows.   *EXCELLENT*
WALLOWA-WHITMAN NATIONAL FORESTS, 2,285-207 acres, Baker, Ore. Trout.   *GOOD*
WILLAMETTE NATIONAL FOREST, 1,666,036 acres, Eugene, Ore. Trout.   *FAIR*

PENNSYLVANIA
ALLEGHENY NATIONAL FOREST, 470,197 acres, Warren, Pa. Trout, bass.   *GOOD*

SOUTH CAROLINA
FRANCIS MARION NATIONAL FOREST, 245,650 acres, Columbia, S. C. Bass.   *GOOD*
SUMTER NATIONAL FOREST, 341,624 acres, Columbia, S. C. Trout, bass.   *GOOD*

SOUTH DAKOTA

BLACK HILLS NATIONAL FOREST, partly in Wyoming, 1,045,441 acres, Custer, S. D. Trout.   *GOOD*

TENNESSEE

CHEROKEE NATIONAL FOREST, 595,097 acres, Cleveland, Tenn. Rainbow, brook trout.   *GOOD*

TEXAS

ANGELINA NATIONAL FOREST, 154,392 acres, Lufkin, Tex. Bass, catfish.   *GOOD*

DAVY CROCKET NATIONAL FOREST, 161,556 acres, Lufkin, Tex. Bass, catfish.   *GOOD*

SABINE NATIONAL FOREST, 183,842 acres, Lufkin, Tex. Bass and catfish.   *GOOD*

SAM HOUSTON NATIONAL FOREST, 158,204 acres, Lufkin, Tex. Catfish, bass.   *GOOD*

UTAH

ASHLEY NATIONAL FOREST, 1,282,829 acres, Vernal, Utah. Trout.   *FAIR*

CACHE NATIONAL FOREST, partly in Idaho, 651,909 acres, Longon, Utah. Trout.   *FAIR*

DIXIE NATIONAL FOREST, 1,839,547 acres, Cedar City, Utah. Trout.   *FAIR*

FISHLAKE NATIONAL FOREST, 1,415,673 acres, Richfield, Utah. Trout.   *GOOD*

MANTI-LA SAL NATIONAL FOREST, partly in Colorado, 1,237,128 acres, Price, Utah. Trout.   *GOOD*

UINTA NATIONAL FOREST, 774,721 acres, Provo, Utah. Trout.   *FAIR*

WASATCH NATIONAL FOREST, partly in Wyoming, 827,441 acres, Salt Lake City, Utah. Holds 576 miles of streams, 115 lakes. Trout.   *GOOD*

VERMONT

GREEN MOUNTAIN NATIONAL FOREST, 230,954 acres, Rutland, Vt. Trout.   *VERY GOOD*

VIRGINIA

GEORGE WASHINGTON NATIONAL FOREST, partly in West Virginia, 1,002,167 acres, Harrisonburg, Va. Trout, bass.   *GOOD*

JEFFERSON NATIONAL FOREST, 542,725 acres, Roanoke, Va. Bass.   *GOOD*

WASHINGTON

COLVILLE NATIONAL FOREST, 928,332 acres, Colville, Wash. Trout.   *FAIR*

GIFFORD PINCHOT NATIONAL FOREST, 1,263,380 acres, Vancouver, Wash. Trout, smallmouth bass.
GOOD

MOUNT BAKER NATIONAL FOREST, 1,818,283 acres, Bellingham, Wash. Steelheads, rainbows. *EXCELLENT*

OKANOGAN NATIONAL FOREST, 1,520,340 acres, Okanogan, Wash. Trout.   *GOOD*

OLYMPIC NATIONAL FOREST, 621,744 acres, Olympia, Wash. Pacific salmon, steelheads, rainbows.
EXCELLENT

SNOQUALMIE NATIONAL FOREST, 1,207,815 acres, Seattle, Wash. Pacific salmon, steelheads, trout.
EXCELLENT

WENATCHEE NATIONAL FOREST, 1,728,086 acres, Wenatchee, Wash. Trout.   *GOOD*

WEST VIRGINIA

MONONGAHELA NATIONAL FOREST, 805,668 acres, Elkins, W. Va. Trout and bass.   *EXCELLENT*

WISCONSIN

CHEQUAMEGON NATIONAL FOREST, 827,027 acres, Park Falls, Wis. Muskellunge.   *GOOD*

NICOLET NATIONAL FOREST, 640,075 acres, Rhinelander, Wis. Muskellunge, pike, bass, trout.
EXCELLENT

This Rolex Watch is self winding, completely waterproof and shockproof.

WYOMING

BIGHORN NATIONAL FOREST, 1,113,597 acres, Sheridan, Wyo. Trout.   *GOOD*

BRIDGER NATIONAL FOREST, 1,699,059 acres, Kemmerer, Wyo. Trout.   *EXCELLENT*

MEDICINE BOW NATIONAL FOREST, 1,063,537 acres, Laramie, Wyo. Trout.   *GOOD*

SHOSHONE NATIONAL FOREST, 2,429,510 acres, Cody, Wyo. Trout.   *EXCELLENT*

TETON NATIONAL FOREST, 1,700,766 acres, Jackson, Wyo. Trout.   *GOOD*

Maps and brochures for these areas may be obtained by writing to: Department of the Interior:, Washington, D.C. Ask for the National Forest area you are particularly interested in.

*Note: Conditions unknown where not noted.

GLOSSARY

ANTI-REVERSE—Mechanism which allows line to be pulled from reel with handle remaining set.

AQUATIC INSECTS—Thos born in the stream or lake and hatched to return to lay eggs, such as stone flies, mayflies, caddis flies.

BACKLASH—Line rolling over itself backwards due to reel spool over-spinning.

BAIT FISHING—Fishing with bait such as worms, minnows.

BAIT CASTING—A term used to describe the casting of plugs or lures which imitate bait fish.

BALANCED TACKLE—Tackle which balances well in hand and also that which, properly selected, performs to its ultimate.

BASS BUG ROD—A staunch fly rod heavier than the usual trout weight to cast heavy bass flies and bug imitations long distances.

CREEL—Willow basket or canvas bag that hold the caught fish.

DRAG—On reel, controls the line flow from the reel spool.

FLIES, ARTIFICIAL—Those made to represent insects and bait fish on which the game fish feed.

GAME FISH—Designated fish species known for their gamy fighting qualities and also those under conservation law protection.

LEVEL WIND MECHANISM—Winds the line on the reel spool evenly without the aid of the guiding fingers of your hand.

NON-MULTIPLYING REEL—Single action, that is one revolution of the spool to one of the handle

OFFSET HANDLE—Handle with the reef seat offset for better positioning for ease in fishing.

PANFISH—Small fish that fit in the frying pan.

SINGLE ACTION REEL—Non-multiplying.

SNAP SWIVEL—A swivel with a snap attached to it for attaching leaders, or additional terminal tackle or lures.

STRIKING—Pulling sharply on the line against the hit of a fish in order to set the hook in his mouth.

TAPERED LEADERS—Almost transparent leaders attached to the line and the end lure that taper from thick to thin in order to make the cast balance out in the air and float down on the water with minimum of disturbance (fly fishing only).

TAPERED LINES—Lines tapered from thick to thin to balance the line in the air for best casting (fly fishing only).

TERMINAL TACKLE—That which is attached to the end of the line, leaders, spreaders, sinkers, hooks, bobbers, lures.

THUMBING THE REEL—Controlling the outgo of the line by pressing on the spool during the cast (bait casting only).

TROLLING—Dragging the bait or lure behind a moving boat.

ULTRA LIGHT TACKLE—The lightest and sportiest tackle practical for fishing conditions and fish species.

BIBLIOGRAPHY

Bates, Jr.. Joseph D.: STREAMER FLY FISHING. New York, D. Van Nostrand Co., 1950.

Bergman, Ray: TROUT. New York, Alfred A. Knopf, 1959.

Brooks, Joe: COMPLETE BOOK OF FLY FISHING. New York, A. S. Barnes & Co., 1958.

Brown, Roderick Haig: FISHERMAN'S WINTER. New York, William Morrow & Co., 1954.

Bueno, Bill: AMERICAN FISHERMAN'S GUIDE. New York, Prentice-Hall, Inc., 1952.

Caine, Lou S.: NORTH AMERICAN FRESH WATER SPORT FISH. New York, A. S. Barnes & Co., 1949.

Camp, Raymond R.: FISHING THE SURF. Boston, Little, Brown & Co., 1950.

Cannon, Raymond: HOW TO FISH THE PACIFIC COAST. Menlo Park, Lane Publishing Co., 1956.

Evanoff, Vlad: SURF FISHING. New York, The Ronald Press Co., 1958.

Farrington, Jr., S. Kip: FISHING THE ATLANTIC. New York, Coward-McCann, Inc., 1949.

LaBranch, George M. L.: THE DRY FLY & FAST WATER. New York, Charles Scribner's Sons, 1914.

La Monte, Francesca: MARINE GAME FISHES OF THE WORLD. New York, Doubleday & Co., 1952.

McClane, A. J.: THE AMERICAN ANGLER. New York, Henry Holt & Co., 1951.

National Geographic Magazine: THE BOOK OF FISHES, 1952.

Quick, Jim: FISHING THE NYMPH. New York, The Ronald Press Co., 1960.

Ritz, Charles: A FLY FISHER'S LIFE. New York, Henry Holt & Co., 1959.

Rodman, O. H. P.: HANDBOOK OF SALT WATER FISHING. Philadelphia, J. B. Lippincott Co., 1952.

Wulff, Lee: ATLANTIC SALMON. New York, A. S. Barnes & Co., 1958.

INDEX

A

Alaska, 24, 35
American angler, 12
Androscoggin River, 21
Atlantic salmon, 29, 35, 36, 40
Atlantic salmon flies, 29
Atlantic salmon tackle, 30

B

Backlash, 12
Baitcasting, 11, 12, 26, 56, 57, 64
Bamboo, 12
Bass, 26, 43
Bass baits, 45
Bass bagging, 16, 69
Bass fishing areas, 44
Beaverkill, 13
Blacker, Wm., 12
Books, 11, Bibliography
British Columbia, 37
Brook trout, 21, 23, 24
Brown trout, 24

C

Cahill fly, 20
California, 37
Chain pickerel, 46
Chinook salmon, 36
Colorado River, 19

D

Delaware River, 13
Documents, 1
Dry flies, 70

F

Fishing information, 78
Fixed spool, 16
Fly casting, 54, 56, 65
Fly-in lakes, 49
Fly rod, 12, 16, 26

G

Gafflines, 45
Gill, Emlyn, 13
Golfers, 53
Gordon, Theo., 13, 17
Green, A. E., 12
Gresham Grits, 17, 51

H

Halford, W. M., 13
Hewitt, Edward, 13, 17
Horrocks-Ibbotson, 12
Huck Finn, 60, 66

I

Ichthyologist, 12, 43

J

Jennings, Preston, 13

K

Kennebec, 27
Kennedy, President, 20
King salmon, 36

L

Labrador, 30
La Branche, 13, 17
Lancer-Leger, 16
Landlocked salmon, 21, 23
Large water bass, 13
Leonard, H. L., 12

M

Maine, 32, 35
Mathieu, Paul, 21, 23
May flies, 19, 23, 24
Meek reel, 12
Mitchell, Wm., 12
Moose River, 23
Murphy, Charles, 12

N

New Brunswick, 31, 35
Newfoundland, 31
New York State Conservation Department, 21
Northern Pike fishing, 46
Nova Scotia, 31
Nymph, 24

O

Oregon, 37
Orvis, Charles, 12
Ovington, Ray, 17

P

Pacific salmon, 35, 36
Pike, 26, 43, 46, 48
Plugs, 72

Q

Quebec, 31

R

Rainbow trout, 21, 23, 24, 60
Rosko, Milt, 17, 60

S

Salmon flies, 27
Seville, Jack, 17, 74
Silver salmon, 36
Skues, G. E. M., 13
Snake River, 24
Snyder, George, 11
Spinning, 13, 26, 57, 58, 61
Spinning lures, 71
Steelhead, 40
Stevens, James, 12
Streamer flies, 23, 68
Suwannee bass, 43

T

Tackle dealers, 75
Tackle tricks, 45
Tapered lines, 66
Trout, 19, 21, 26

W

Washington, 37
Worms, 24
Wulff, Lee, 27

Z

Zwirz, Bob, 11, 54

The Compact Book
of Fresh Water Fishing

The Compact Outdoorsman's Library

Ray Ovington
Editor-in-Chief

Editorial Advisory Board

Jack Seville, Milt Rosko, Bob Zwirz,
Tom McNally, Grits Gresham, Sid Latham,
Van Ellman, John Falk, Jim Rikhoff,
Clyde Ormond, Gene Hill

Publication Schedule

The Compact Book of Boating, Edited by Jack Seville

The Compact Book of Fresh Water Fishing, Edited by Bob Zwirz

The Compact Book of Outdoor Photography, Edited by Ray Ovington

The Compact Book of Hunting, Edited by Jim Rikhoff

75 cents each

Forthcoming titles will include books on
*Water Skiing, Scuba and Skin Diving,
Archery, Salt Water Fishing, Figure Skating,
and Horseback Riding.*

J. LOWELL PRATT & COMPANY
Publishers
137 EAST 57TH STREET, NEW YORK 22